Midnight's Diaspora ⌒

Midnight's Diaspora

Critical Encounters with Salman Rushdie

Edited by
Daniel Herwitz and Ashutosh Varshney

THE UNIVERSITY OF MICHIGAN PRESS

Ann Arbor

Copyright © by the University of Michigan 2008
Chapters by Ashutosh Varshney, "The Political Rushdie" and "Lasting
Injuries, Recuperative Possibilities," Copyright © 2008 by author.
All rights reserved
Published in the United States of America by
The University of Michigan Press
Manufactured in the United States of America
⊗ Printed on acid-free paper

2011   2010   2009   2008   4   3   2   1

No part of this publication may be reproduced,
stored in a retrieval system, or transmitted in any form
or by any means, electronic, mechanical, or otherwise,
without the written permission of the publisher.

A CIP catalog record for this book is available from the British Library.

Library of Congress Cataloging-in-Publication Data

Midnight's diaspora : critical encounters with Salman Rushdie / edited
    by Daniel Herwitz and Ashutosh Varshney.
        p.   cm.
    Includes index.
    ISBN-13: 978-0-472-07048-0 (cloth : alk. paper)
    ISBN-10: 0-472-07048-7 (cloth : alk. paper)
    ISBN-13: 978-0-472-05048-2 (pbk. : alk. paper)
    ISBN-10: 0-472-05048-6 (pbk. : alk. paper)
        1. Rushdie, Salman—Criticism and interpretation.   2. Rushdie,
Salman—Interviews.   I. Herwitz, Daniel Alan, 1955–   II. Varshney,
Ashutosh, 1957–
PR6068.U757Z767   2007
823'.914—dc22   2008022950

Contents

Midnight's Diaspora ❧

DANIEL HERWITZ

Introduction

Two decades have passed since Ayatollah Khomeini issued a fatwa against Salman Rushdie. The fatwa, which followed the publication of Rushdie's novel *The Satanic Verses,* consigned the author to a decade in hiding and generated an international furor around freedom of speech and religious offense that has continued to this day. His knighthood in June 2007 produced official condemnation by the Pakistani parliament and a wave of death threats. Throughout it all Rushdie has remained an uncompromising, cosmopolitan, idiomatic, witty voice. A writer who spent his childhood and adolescence in India and Pakistan and yet also possesses an English pedigree straight out of *Tom Brown's School-days,* a fierce critic of Thatcher's England and, more recently, of fundamentalist practices, Rushdie has cut a wide swath across the world. His life has congregated minions and incensed hordes; his pen has remained a lamp and a sword. From early fame with the publication of his second novel, *Midnight's Children,* in 1981 (about the twin experiences of Indian independence and Indo-Pakistani partition), to the stories of Pakistan *(Shame)* and of Thatcher's England *(The Satanic Verses),* from those written to his son while in hiding *(Haroun and the Sea of Stories)* to the ongoing melodrama of a Bombay now wracked by riot of conflagration *(The Moor's Last Sigh),* and more recently, his account of Elvis and John Lennon in New York and the final entry into the diaspora *(The Ground beneath Her Feet),* his lyric voice has sought to fictionalize torrential times.

Given the decades that have unfolded since the fatwa, it is timely to revisit his career and reengage that voice. This book has brought together noted Indian, Pakistani, and European intellectuals to speak to Rushdie's books and the world they are of. When the ground beneath her feet quakes, to adapt one of Rushdie's recent titles, it is because real events have caused skyscrapers to collapse out of the New York skyline and people to die in a hundred venues throughout the world. It is also because Rushdie's storytelling voice has caused the ground that is real life to live in a second, expository place where storytelling converts history into language, and poetry dazzles. Rushdie's fiction is the place where history and story meet, but it is not the only place. For his books can only be as they are because history is already a landscape of dreams, the product of human imagination (sufficient unto the day or insufficient thereof), a ground where people live but also levitate in fiction and fantasy. Real history is already in this sense literature before the fact, literature waiting to happen. Rushdie's career is a study in these facts about history. Rushdie's books celebrate dreaming but also offer insights into the carnage thereby wrought. Given their terrain, they lead directly to all manner of questions about morality, human rights, philosophy, and politics. Our authors take up these questions, surveying India, Pakistan, global politics, and philosophical morality in the light of Rushdie's work.

Rushdie tells us in his response to our authors that he speaks about his work only because he has been forced to do so by the communalizing, destructive responses it has received—often from people who have never read it. It is now twenty years after the fatwa and so worth remembering that *The Satanic Verses* retells the story of Muhammad for a specific purpose: because the main characters in that book can only be plane-crashed into Thatcher's England (with its riot and racism) if they've been displaced from tradition, lost terrain. They become diaspora because they've exited Malabar Hill, Bombay, but also because they've lost the direct inheritance of the stories and truths they once believed, in particular the story of Muhammad. This is a condition of modern life and its discontents that fundamentalism refuses to acknowledge: that the truths of the past must be recovered through an act of interpretation because we've been crashed out of them. There is no judgment about the quality and character of those truths in *The Satanic Verses;* Rushdie is a writer, not a theologian. What Rushdie has done is sketch the way fictional characters lose homeland and home story, and what it is like to live in those circumstances.

Ironically, of course, the fatwa made Rushdie a celebrity. His celebrity status comes from his trauma (ten years in hiding from fanaticism and fatwa), and from his lively screen presence. It bespeaks the voraciousness of the star system, the way that the media system harps on trauma and converts it into public fixation. Rushdie is, from the point of view of the media, amazingly similar to Jackie, Marilyn, Diana Princess of Wales, each of whom entered the silvery light of the silver screen through a combination of star quality and life trauma—trauma that played itself out before the gaze of millions. The public hankered for the next chapter in the Diana story in something of the degree of fixation it had while waiting to find what would happen to Salman Rushdie. The Earl of Spenser, Diana's brother, described Diana's as "the most bizarre life imaginable" in his funeral oration. The same words could be used about Rushdie's last two decades. The amazing thing is that Rushdie has embraced the potentially disfiguring challenge of his celebrity status and used his notoriety for more than cash value: to tell it like it is, attack the depth of the lie against a tide of placating media responses and crazed Internet web sites (not to mention sermons), to become public intellectual as well as literary writer. The various essays, short pieces, and public appearances in which Rushdie has done this prove that it is still possible to write for the media without reducing language to aspirin—and be published as well. Rushdie has written on a wide range of topics—including 9/11, the Middle East, India, the fate of women, and human rights—with a fierce, razor-sharp, and mordant turn of phrase. He has become a kind of Sartrean figure, with the one thing Sartre lacked: a self-ironizing sense of the hilarity of the Circus Maximus that is our times and of the even greater absurdity of his own position in the center ring. But then his protagonists have often had that astonishment, that irony, as well.

Our book begins with two interviews Rushdie gave in 2003 in Ann Arbor, Michigan, one political (with Ashutosh Varshney, my coeditor of this volume and professor of political science, University of Michigan), the other literary (with Gauri Viswanathan, professor of English and comparative literature at Columbia University).[1] These interviews show Rushdie at his best: subtle and supple, engaged, and hilarious. They are paeans to the art of free speech. His fine command of the art of free speech does not make the charge of having given offense go away but rather (to his enemies) augments that charge, which is why the opening essay is by a philosopher: Akeel Bilgrami, Jonsonian Professor of Philosophy at Columbia and a long-engaged figure in Muslim politics. Bilgrami was among the first to stand up publicly for Rushdie after the fatwa was decreed (on the *McNeil/Lehrer News Hour*). He is among the few to rethink questions of free speech in a way that includes, indeed addresses, "moderate Muslims," as he puts it. Bilgrami's subtlety is to argue that on the one hand there is no abstract defense of free speech that can prove decisive for such skeptics of that value as Rushdie's moderate Muslim detractors. A viable defense of free speech must show that such skeptics share (something of) the value in spite of their denials. Only if the skeptic realizes that he or she is in something of the same ballpark as the free-speech proponent will it be possible for debate about the details of this value to take place in a way profitable for human practice. Bilgrami also argues that fury against Rushdie among British Muslims is a misdirected response that ought to be vented toward the British state. For British liberalism does exactly what, philosophically, Bilgrami argues is incorrect: it proclaims free speech from the pulpit on high rather than seeking dialogue that would find common ground beneath the feet of both parties. Ashutosh Varshney and Husain Haqqani, advisor to three Pakistani prime ministers, visiting fellow at the Carnegie Center for International Peace, and now Pakistan's ambassador to the United States, each take up the question of Rushdie's Pakistan. Taking as their point of departure an ingenious phrase from Rushdie's *Shame* that asks whether Pakistan is simply a case of "insufficient imagination," Varshney spins the question toward the future: to what extent is Pakistan capable of reimagining itself, given what the insufficiency has politically been. Pakistan, Varshney reminds us, was born as a Muslim, *not* an Islamic state. Mohammed Jinnah, its founder, was fiercely secular. He saw it as a place of refuge for a civilization distinct from and ever threatened by the Hindu majority in India. Islam the religion was recruited for secular purposes, to become the glue that might hold together in imagination a hugely divided set of Muslim communities, something Husain Haqqani also discusses in his essay. As these divisions began to break through to the surface in the history of Pakistan, however, Islam became the central ideology through which the state was imagined. What was originally a secular and cultural source of solidarity was now reasserted in stronger and stronger religious doses. The medicine was, however, the disease, and formerly robust Pakistani liberal traditions were threatened. The barrenness of this history of self-imagination is a key issue for both Varshney and Haqqani, and their respective political analyses are in many ways parallel to those offered in Rushdie's *Shame.*

Thomas Blom Hansen, professor of anthropology at the University of Amsterdam, seeks to uncover and understand the shifting ground of Rushdie's Bombay. Framed by *Midnight's Children,* with its picture of the old, ebullient, impure, magical Bombay of Rushdie's midnight childhood, and *The Moor's Last Sigh,* which takes place in the Bombay of kerosene, torch and Shiv Sena riots, Hansen's essay addresses two key questions that these two books together raise. First, how could that city have changed so precipitously? Second, and related to the first: what has this violence really been about? Who are its true discontents? His answers delve into urban history, sectors of impoverishment, long-standing social resentment, and the theory of sovereignty.

Sara Suleri Goodyear, professor of comparative literature at Yale University and author of a noted memoir on Pakistan, skillfully unfolds, thread by thread, the multiple meanings of the veil in Rushdie's books. From this singular image she teases out metaphors of partition, the separateness of women, the broad swatch of Pakistan, the silk-screen semiautonomy that is literature itself. Behind the veil you are autonomous—or at least may believe yourself to be so—even if you are regarded by others as confined. The veil is a place where abundance of vision may take place but also the terror of separation. It is a word and image that is paradigmatic of what she (spicily) calls Rushdie's "chutnification of language." The silken, sultry quality of her essay veils its controversial nature.

Shashi Tharoor, fiction writer of note and until recently undersecretary-general for communications and public information at the United Nations, takes as his topic not a chutney but a plate: the *thali*. The *thali* is a meal of many distinctive, small foods, elegantly arranged on a large platter so as to offer a prism of tastes for the palate. And, according to Tharoor, the *thali* has also been a metaphor for the Indian nation. Unity in diversity, many into one, single polyglot nation, place of singular multiplicity: "The singular thing about India is that you can only speak of it in the plural," he says, and this pluralism has served both as a state ideology (for the Congress Party) and a cultural image for a country where less than 50 percent speak the "national language." Tharoor's essay dovetails nicely with Husain Haqqani's, in which he reminds us of the following passage from Rushdie's *Shame:* "It is well known that the term 'Pakistan,' an acronym, was originally thought up in England by a group of Muslim intellectuals. P for the Punjabis, A for the Afghans, K for the Kashmiris, S for Sind and the 'tan,' they say, for Baluchistan." For, as the passage implies, the invention of unity within multiplicity is both fantasy and a genuine state process. The strong arm of the Congress Party claimed to deliver social welfare by enforcing strict conformity of states to the national agenda. In Pakistan the very question of governability, given all manner of political, social, and geographical diversity, is central. This ungovernability is the starting point, Tharoor shows us, of Rushdie's language, of his literary project, for Rushdie feasts on the fiesta of polyglot, polygamous languages, he Saul Bellows them into boisterous storytelling with the bellowing voice of a Towering Babel, babbling with the fluency of an historical river of perpetual infancy (and sometimes, infanticide). In keeping with Tharoor's characterization, Rushdie himself has a lot to say about the importance of American Jewish writing (Roth and Bellow) for his own work in his interview with Gauri Viswanathan. Rushdie is, Tharoor suggests, "the most gifted reinventor of Indianness since Nehru." If so, then the ability to convert reality into story is a central part of this magic property. Although Tharoor does not take up the point, such a property of Indianness has a dark side. That central Indian personage, the storyteller, has been known to make up stories of India that lay the ground for the devastation of other Indians. This is what we see represented in *The Moor's Last Sigh,* a novel about nationalist violence and abrogating terror. How strong is the dark side then, of this mythical property, this national fantasy?

This hard question, so central to Rushdie's work and to the essays in this volume, is not one to which we can presume to offer a definitive answer: history is a ground that will continue to shift just at the moment we consider it stable enough to venture the words. Our book—published twenty years after the fatwa—may soon enough find itself out of date in its approach to this and many other questions. However, it can at least be said that the themes of this book—the global writer's creation of linguistic idiom, fiction's relation to fact, the wizardry and warp of Indian and Pakistani history, the question of Muslim identity and U.S. policy, the freedom of women and their veils, and finally, freedom of speech and the ongoing quality of the imagination that goes into it—remain themes for our times. This book's encounter with Rushdie will be salient so long as these themes continue to captivate human history.

NOTE

1. The current volume consists of articles on his literary and public intellectual voice and formation, along with a pair of interviews he gave on the occasion of what can only be another gesture of celebrity, the Royal Shakespeare Company's performance of the theater version of his *Midnight's Children* at the University of Michigan in 2003. The unlikely majesty of *Midnight's Children*'s ending up on stage was the result of the same celebrity notoriety that has come to define Rushdie's public life for the past twenty years or more. Rushdie had written a screenplay based on the novel that was supposed to be made into a film in India, until it was axed for a reason any reader of this volume could easily work out. Censorship proved ironically felicitous for the University of Michigan, since the theater work that *Midnight's Children* became in its second incarnation ended up performed by the Royal Shakespeare Company in its second Ann Arbor residency in 2003, and with Salman Rushdie also present. It was that event which ultimately led to the interviews and some of the essays in this volume.

Cynthia Middleton, Marysia Ostafin, and Michael Kennedy are happily thanked for their organizational support. The Office of the President, University of Michigan; the University Musical Society; the Center for South Asian Studies; and the Institute for the Humanities (which I direct) hosted the Rushdie event.

Interviews with Salman Rushdie ❧

The Political Rushdie

An Interview by Ashutosh Varshney

This public interview, hitherto unpublished, was conducted by Ashutosh Varshney on March 12, 2003, at the University of Michigan, Ann Arbor. It was the first of several public events that formed part of the festival that premiered Midnight's Children *as a play in the United States under the direction of the Royal Shakespeare Company. The interview lasted nearly two hours, and close to two thousand people thronged the auditorium to watch and hear it.*

Ashutosh Varshney: In one of the reviews in the *Times Literary Supplement* (TLS), *Midnight's Children* was called an example of Salman Rushdie's "amazing inventiveness."[1] The reviewer also said the following "In *Midnight's Children* talking outdoes doing. The book is held together by the voice of its charming, garrulous narrator, whose manic intimacy hooks attention even when swarms of events and characters threaten to derail it." And, finally, the book was also called an unparalleled example of "the exuberance of Rushdie's cultural cross-dressing." These formulations and many others are about the literary craft of *Midnight's Children,* but my task today is not to concentrate on these literary aspects. I am a political scientist, with a specialization in South Asian politics, and I would, therefore, like to focus on the political Rushdie.

Why should we talk about the political Rushdie at all? Why should we not entirely abandon Salman Rushdie to the literary scholars and critics? The reason is quite simple. Rushdie is an intense political being. He has often claimed that political context plays a significant role in his storytelling and artistic imagination. Consider briefly *Midnight's Children* as well as some other Rushdie novels. Through its events, characters, and stories, *Midnight's Children* covers a long and significant period of South Asian politics—1918 to 1978. After the Amritsar Massacre of April 1919 led by a British general, Reginald Dyer, Mahatma Gandhi burst on the scene, and India's freedom movement under his leadership plunged into mass politics. Politics before Gandhi was primarily an elite affair. India's leaders used to make constitutional argu-

9

ments against their British rulers in the Queen's English. Gandhi mobilized the masses, used nonelite idioms of politics, preferred civil disobedience over legal and constitutional arguments, and made the freedom movement stronger. Mass politics has been a continuing feature of Indian politics ever since. The novel's end also roughly coincides with a significant political landmark—the end of the only formally dictatorial period of postindependence India, the period of Emergency (1975–77), headed by Mrs. Indira Gandhi.

Rushdie's other novels are also steeped in politics. Military generals play an important role in *Shame,* his novel about Pakistan, or "a novel about a place not quite Pakistan," as he playfully described it. Finally, Hindu nationalist politics constitutes an important part of *The Moor's Last Sigh,* a novel published in 1995.

To those who study the politics and history of the Indian subcontinent, as I do with many others, it is transparent that Salman Rushdie's novels as well as his nonfiction are highly political. Indeed, that is why scholars of politics are so irresistibly drawn to his work. He seems to be singularly incapable of telling a story without political sharpness, without political courage, sometimes at great personal risk, as all of us know. Governments get involved with him, religious leaders get involved with him, and his work has touched off political demonstrations. Hence the title of this interview, "The Political Rushdie."

So let us start our political conversation.

Salman Rushdie: Could I tell you a story about Indira Gandhi? I never met Indira Gandhi, but clearly she does not come out well in *Midnight's Children.* When the book was first submitted to the publishers in India, they were quite nervous that the book was rude about the prime minister of India. I was asked to provide a justification for the various statements made about the Emergency, and about Mrs. Gandhi's part in it, and I had to write a long letter to the publishers, explaining my statements. When the book came out and after it won the Booker Prize, I received a phone call from No. 10 Downing Street, from Margaret Thatcher's office. It was to invite me to a lunch that Mrs. Thatcher was giving in honor of Indira Gandhi. I said, "It really is a joke, right?" And the voice sounded a little flustered and said, "What do you mean exactly?" I said, "Well, you know, I wrote this book." He said, "We are talking about *Midnight's Children?*" I said, "Yes, that is right." "And you won the Booker Prize?" "Yes, yes." "Well you see the Foreign Office recommended you. We haven't really read your book, but we thought the Foreign Office would have read it." I said, "Well, it is just that Mrs. Gandhi would not be very pleased if I showed up for a lunch in her honor." Anyway, to cut a long story short, they were caught in a terrible situation. If they withdrew the invitation, then I could get them for that, but if they did not withdraw the invitation, then that would be a different kind of problem. In any case I thought I would find it rather odd to be at the luncheon, so I said, "Well, you know, I have been thinking about it and I probably won't come." There was this incredible relief on the other end of the phone. The voice said, "Oh, of course, if that is how you feel. Perhaps you could come on some other occasion." I was never asked to come on any other occasion.

Anyway, three years after the book came out, Mrs. Gandhi tried to sue me. There is one sentence in *Midnight's Children,* a complete background sentence, in which I'm talking about her earlier career. The sentence talks about her relationship with her son, Sanjay Gandhi, and why he supposedly had so much power over her. And it repeats a well-known story of the time, which is that Sanjay Gandhi had always blamed his mother for causing the death of his father by an early heart attack. You know they separated and so on, and his father, Feroze Gandhi, died after his separation from Indira Gandhi. Sanjay had blamed Indira for that and as a result she felt guilty, and she therefore could not deny him anything.

This was a story that many people had circulated all over India. It had been often published, and in the novel it is reported as a rumor. It is not that I am saying this is what happened; I am saying this is what people used to say. Anyway, Mrs Gandhi sued about this sentence. In the letter I had written to the publishers three years previously, I had said that this is the only sentence in the book that I could not justify— because it is about three people: two of them are dead and the third is the one who would be suing you. But I said it has been in the public domain, it has often been published before, so I don't see any problems with it. That letter saved my life because it meant that the publishers had accepted that as the basis of publication, so they couldn't repudiate me.

We had in retrospect a very funny meeting with a very senior lawyer in England to discuss the defense. He said, "The law of defamation is highly technical and in theory if you repeat a defamation, even if you say it is a rumor, you actually commit the defamation with the equal force of the original defamation. Otherwise you could defame anybody by saying it is a rumor. So in theory she is right, this is defamatory." To be fair, however, she was not being very hostile, was not asking for damages, was not asking for the book to be withdrawn. She was asking that in future printings of the book, that sentence should be removed. That was the extent of her request. I said to the lawyer, "I am not the lawyer, you're the lawyer. What I know is that there is always a defense. So what is the defense?" He said, "Well, in order to defame an individual, that person has to be a person of good character. So if you could show to me why the prime minister of India is not a woman of good character, then we have got a defense." . . . This line of reasoning was quite remarkable.

In the end, I said, "Look the thing that worries me is that this is actually an unimportant sentence, its really just background, it has nothing to do with the story. But what I don't want is for her to come back and then sue again about another sentence and then another sentence, and so on. So it has to be a once-and-for-all settlement. And I said that if she would agree that this was the sum total of her complaint against the book, then actually we've won. Because what it means is that she is telling us is that she has no complaint with the description of the Emergency. The lawyer said, "That is quite right, and we would not accept a settlement except if she agreed that that was the sum total of her complaint."

As a result, every Indian newspaper ran front-page stories, something like, "Mrs. Gandhi Agrees with Mr. Rushdie's Description of the Emergency." So we had agreed to take that sentence out of the reprints, but then she was murdered. And you can't libel the dead.

Freedom to Speak, Freedom to Offend

AV: The website announcing the events of this week at the University of Michigan opens with a quote from you. And the quote is, "What is freedom of expression? Without the freedom to offend, it ceases to exist." Political philosophers have long debated whether freedom of expression has any legitimate boundaries. And at least some liberal political theorists who are committed to free speech—someone like Isaiah Berlin—might still make a distinction between the freedom to criticize and the freedom to offend. This is something that legal theory also pays attention to. Do you find this analytic distinction between criticism and offense relevant to the world of novelists and artists?

SR: I don't, but let me tell you why. Because first of all I don't know what is going to offend people. I get offended all the time. Bad sentences offend me. All sorts of people's political opinions offend me—they're on television every day. My view in general is that democracy is not a polite business, it is not a tea party. Democracy is often the clash of violently differing opinions. One man's ideology is another man's offense. You can't have a free conversation about ideas without offending some people.

One of the strange things about free speech is that if you live in a society which, broadly speaking, has free speech, you don't think about it that often. It's like if there is enough air to breathe, you do not think about the air. When somebody starts turning off the tap, you suddenly start noticing that air is important. I got much more involved in the subject of free speech after somebody tried to take away mine. And it made me understand that the defense of freedom of speech precisely begins at the point at which somebody says something that offends you. It doesn't end at that point.

I'll give you an example: After *The Satanic Verses* was published, a movie was made in Pakistan called *International Guerrillas,* of which I was the villain. And the international guerrillas were proto-Aryan kind of mujahideen heroes, whose job it was to kill me. One of the things that really offended me was that I was depicted as always having a bottle of whisky in my hand, and a kind of whip in the other, sometimes a sword lurching around.

AV: With women on your side also.

SR: Oh, there were all kinds of people in various stages of undress, but you know a Pakistani movie is so not very undressed. I was being guarded by what looked like the Israeli Secret Service, and there was a moment in this film where they captured one of these international guerrillas. He was strung between two palm trees, and I was drinking whisky and whipping him in turn. There was also a scene of incredible unintentional comedy where, after I had tortured him for a little while, I turned to the Israeli Secret Service and said, "Take him away and read to him from *The Satanic Verses* all night!" And he went, "Not that, anything but that!" Anyway, at the end of this film I do get killed. I get killed by a bolt of lightning.

The film was brought to England and they sought a certificate for it. In many ways, the film was inflammatory and I obviously had a case against it. So the British Board of Film Classification, as it is called, refused it a certificate. I was in this odd situation where I was fighting a free-speech battle, but being defended by an act of censorship. One of the reasons they did not issue a certificate was simply that, according to their lawyers, I could easily sue them. If they gave it a certificate, they would become party to the defamation, as in the Indira Gandhi case. Therefore, by allowing the defamation to be seen they would be guilty of defamation too. In the end, I had to write this surrealist letter to the board, giving up my right of legal defense, saying that I formally would not sue. I asked them to give the film its certificate, saying that I did not wish to be protected by an act of censorship.

The film was given a certificate, and the producers booked the biggest theater in Bradford, a town with the largest Muslim population in England, in Yorkshire. Nobody went to see the film. A complete flop, it had to be taken off after two or three days. It was a fantastic vindication of the free-speech position, which is that people can make up their own minds. So that is why I am saying you have to defend the stuff you can't stand, and you have to trust the good judgment of the public to make up their minds about it.

AV: Well, this story does raise some related issues. In the early nineteenth century, James Mill, while writing the history of British India, called Indians "imbecile brutes" who had no history of their own. And he also said that if Indians wanted to claim that in ancient and medieval times they had made a lot of scientific achievements in numerology, in astronomy, et cetera, it was, according to Mill, simply a typical act of Indian perfidy and deceit. Similarly, in much of the literature of a certain time, you find very demeaning descriptions of African Americans, of women, of the ex-untouchables in India, so and so forth. If the powerful are making offensive assertions about the subaltern, there has to be some way for a society to deal with it.

SR: Oh yes, the answer is to answer back. The point I am making is that the ideas don't cease to exist if you suppress their expression. Those ideas are there in society, reprehensible and ugly as they may be. It seems to me much better to have them out in the open, where you can argue with them and demolish them, than to have them under the carpet.

AV: Feminists might say you needed some kind of legal protection before feminists could speak out freely about gender issues. You needed some sort of legal protection before black Americans could speak out freely about the demeaning images of their community.

SR: I was around when the women's movement got going. I don't remember Germaine Greer asking for legal protection.

AV: Okay, so your point is that those who are offended by that speech have to mobilize opinion, or political support, and hit back.

SR: Yeah, I mean hit back in the form of speech.

India and Pakistan

AV: Let us move on to some South Asia–specific questions. From your work, people have inferred that your relationship with India is one of great fondness. Here is what you wrote in 2000, when you visited India after a gap of twelve to thirteen years, a separation forced by the fatwa: "I have left India many times. The first time was when I was thirteen and a half and went to boarding school in Rugby, England. . . . Since then my characters have frequently flown west from India, but in novel after novel their author's imagination has returned to it. This perhaps is what it means to love a country: that its shape is also yours, the shape of the way you think, feel, and dream. That you can never really leave." In contrast, your relationship with Pakistan is shot through with considerable ambivalence. India animates your work much more than Pakistan does. In *Midnight's Children,* Saleem Sinai loses his telepathic powers when he gets to Pakistan from India. In *Shame* one gets the feeling that the sentence that Pakistan is a "failure of the dreaming mind" is a sentence that betrays your own position about that country. Do you feel a sense of ambivalence about Pakistan? How would you define your relationship with Pakistan?

SR: Yes, I don't like Pakistan.

AV: Would you explain why? What's the source of that?

SR: Obviously I like lots of people there, but . . .

AV: But nearly half of your family lived there. Half lived in India and the other half lived . . .

SR: Oh yes, absolutely. You know for somebody who grew up in India—of all places, actually in Bombay in the fifties and sixties—to go from there to Karachi felt like you were suddenly going to a world of incredible difference. In those days the problems had more to do with dictatorship than with religious issues. But it felt unfree if you were used to living in a free society, which India, broadly speaking, was. Then there was the growth of Islamization, which narrowed the society even more.

I did say Pakistan was insufficiently imagined, that it was a failure of the dreaming mind. The proof of that is Bangladesh. You have this country, carved out of the subcontinent based on religious principles. You have a chunk over here and a chunk over there. Saleem in *Midnight's Children* has a line where he describes Pakistan as this strange bird with two wings without a body. The religious basis for the state was an insufficient glue, and other resentments began to take precedence over that. East Pakistanis felt quite rightly oppressed by West Pakistan. There was a great deal of racial bigotry between West Pakistan and East Pakistan. Racist terms were very commonly in use in West Pakistan.

AV: Actually President Ayub himself wrote in a very racist way about Bengali Muslims in *Friends, Not Masters*.

SR: Yeah, and East Pakistan was treated as a colony of West Pakistan. The idea that Islam was a sufficient glue to hold the country together was demonstrated to be empty. Even now if you look at Pakistan, the regional resentments are colossal. So that was my problem—it's a country that doesn't work. It is also a country in which, unlike India, the institutions of a free society have never been allowed to take root. In India, the Emergency, one and a half years long, was the only time that the system veered away from elections. Meanwhile, in Pakistan you had either a succession of military dictatorships or civilian governments of intense corruption backed by the army, which was always waiting in the wings to take over if the civilians went too far. That's the tragedy of Pakistan, that when you get rid of a general, you get a civilian politician who is corrupt, and then you get another general and then you get another corrupt civilian politician and then you get another general. It is a catastrophe of a political system. So of course I don't like it as much as India.

Life in Bombay

AV: Let us now turn to Bombay. Thomas Blom Hansen, a professor of social anthropology at Yale, has done two books on Bombay. He gave a talk here recently entitled "Reflections on Rushdie's Bombay."[2] He greatly admired you as a novelist, but his basic argument was that your view of Bombay was rosy, romantic, and starry-eyed. Though you do, of course, concede the decline of Bombay's civil and political fabric in your more recent work, the fact remains that even while you were growing up in Bombay, 1947 through 1962–63, when you left for Rugby, England, Bombay had two sides: the lovely, multicultural, cosmopolitan world of the upper classes, and—I think these are his words—the nasty, mafia-infested slums and plebeian quarters in which the teeming millions lived. The great difference today, argues Hansen, is that in all sorts of barely disguised ways, the mafia, the dons, the crime syndicate have arrived at the center of political stage and at the center of Bollywood, another aspect of Bombay that really fascinates you and is so much part of your work. Any comments?

SR: Well, there is some justice in that. There is no question that Bombay has become a much darker place than what it was in the fifties and early sixties. Bombay was always a city full of poor people, and, of course, there were always slums, and there was organized crime. It would be absurd to pretend otherwise. But it has become much, much worse. The gulf between wealth and poverty, always extreme in Bombay, has become much greater. Much greater wealth, much greater poverty. The growth in the slums has been explosive because of the arrival of many more millions of people from the rest of India to Bombay. The growth of sectarianism has been enormously fostered by the emergence of groups like the Shiv Sena, and the criminal mafias, very largely Muslim. One of the interesting untold stories of Bombay is the battle between the political gangs and the criminal gangs. The political gangs are all fundamentalist Hindus, and the criminal gangs are all Muslim. So you have Hindu-Muslim struggle at the level of the mafia. The Bombay of the fifties and sixties lacked religious sectarianism. That is the big difference between Bombay then and Bombay now. Like so many people, like the family of Saleem in *Midnight's Children,* like my own family, Muslims saw Bombay as a safe place during the partition massacre.

AV: And that is why your family left Delhi to be in Bombay.

SR: Well, they left in 1945–46. In the novel, Saleem's family leaves very close to partition. My family actually left earlier. But substantially yes, a lot of Muslim families knew that Delhi was going to be difficult, and indeed it was very dangerous. In Bombay essentially nothing happened at partition. And the people of Bombay, as I was growing up, took great pride that the city was tolerant and cosmopolitan. Yes, I came from a wealthy family, and of course, it was much easier in that part of society. But even at the level of the masses, there were no religious riots. The riots that there were in Bombay were language riots. It had to do with Maharashtra, Gujarat, and the separation of the old Bombay state into what are now two states of Maharashtra and Gujarat. Those were the major civil disturbances of the period. Religion was not a contentious issue.

A lot of people that I remember and a lot of people of my parents' generation and writing from that generation refer to that period in the history of Bombay as a kind of special period. The atmosphere of the city was different. After the arrival of Hindu nationalist politics in Bombay, the city changed in character. Now you have a situation where, you know, Muslim families don't like to put their name on the front door of their houses.

I focused in *Midnight's Children* on the lives of the relatively wealthy. But one should say there is the point about having the baby swap, of having the life of Shiva also there in the background. The darkness is there. Shiva's life is spent amongst the gangs. He describes himself as somebody who has been fighting in the gangs. It is at the edges of the little enclave in which Saleem lives his life, but it is not ignored, it is referred to explicitly, and the darkness of that world gradually seeps closer and closer to the center of the action, as the novel darkens towards the end. In the end you just have to let the book be what it is. Yes, it has tinges of romance about it. But I don't think it ignores a reality that was out there.

Novelists and Political Responsibility

AV: Do you think that those novelists who are unmindful of politics, or who simply wish to tell a human story, abdicate a novelist's intellectual and political responsibility. Should novelists be viewed as necessarily having political responsibility?

SR: Something worries me about those words. I don't like to use them because I don't like to be prescriptive for how other writers approach their art. It seems to me people will do what they like, and that's their business. I have always wanted to write a book which wasn't political. The time that I had thought I had nearly done it was *The Satanic Ver-*

sus. I thought it was a very personal book about migration, as I was trying to write about the things that happened in my life. *Midnight's Children* deals with India and the political situation there. *Shame* deals with
Pakistan and the way it grows out of the political crisis there. I thought
this time I would talk about something much less structured by historical events, and much more about internal change. It is a novel about
metamorphosis—the character is physically metamorphosed after all. I
guess I was wrong.

I still think it is not a political novel. It's a novel about the changes
that happen to individuals and communities under the pressure of migration. And it's a novel about London in the 1980s. Its longest central
section is called a "City Visible, Yet Unseen." I wanted to talk about
the immigrant community in London, particularly the South Asian immigrant community, and at that time what I wanted to say about it is,
"Here's this enormous community of people who are, it seems, invisible—their concerns, their lives, you know, their fears, and so on,
somehow invisible to the white population." I wanted to make it visible. And that is one of the ways in which I think England has changed,
because I don't think you could say that about it now. You couldn't say
that the South Asian community was invisible now. That is one of the
ways in which England has changed for the better. But at that time
there was clearly a desire to portray this large, migrant community that
nobody was paying any attention to.

AV: As Amartya Sen puts it, chicken tikka has become a British staple!

SR: Exactly. Let me return to the question of whether novelists have
political responsibilities. I'm saying it is my own instinct, and the reason it's my instinct is that it seems to me that the space between public
life and private life has disappeared. If you look at the novels of Jane
Austen, she was able to spend her entire career fully exploring the lives
of her characters while making almost no reference to the Napoleonic
Wars. When soldiers arrived in Jane Austen's novels, they looked nice
in uniform, and people wanted to dance with them in parties. They
very rarely came back bloodied. The uniforms were always in great
shape. Why were they in great shape? Because in that period Jane
Austen was able to fully explore and explain the lives of her people
without reference to the public dimension. The public dimension was
far away from the lives of the people. So it is not that she was deliberately averting her gaze. It is that she could tell her story completely
without reference to the public dimension. It seems to me now the

space between private life and public life has just vanished. They are up against each other all the time. And, as a result, I have felt as a writer the need to recognize that and therefore to include a discussion of the public dimension.

Popular Culture and Classical Arts

AV: Your novels are full of references to Bollywood, to India's popular culture. The great, centuries-long Indian tradition of classical music or classical dances does not appear prominently in your work. Is your preference for pop culture, or for Bollywood, a political one, in that it allows you to sketch characters and write stories that can reach large audiences? Or is the choice an artistic one, in that the classical Indian art or classical Indian music doesn't really fascinate you and it's Bollywood that grabs your attention?

SR: It is not a political decision. It is not even really a literary decision because I never really expected to have a large audience. When *Midnight's Children* came out, I was first hoping that it would be well received, that people would think it was a good book and so on, and I was delighted when they did. I didn't expect a global best-seller. Until then the only novels about India that had any kind of currency globally had been novels about the Western experience of India. It was often an individual experience like in *Heat and Dust,* somebody going to India and falling in love, and that was almost always with a maharaja. Nobody fell in love with a clerk. There was always a maharaja available.

AV: In the film *Lagaan,* that changed a little.

SR: But that's very recent. I am talking about then. Western experiences of the East, broadly speaking, seemed to be the only way of making the East accessible or interesting to a global audience. *Midnight's Children* was a novel with Indian experiences of India, and nobody had shown any signs of being interested in that outside India before.

But what did I think about Bollywood? Actually, I never called it Bollywood. Nobody called it Bollywood when I was growing up—it is a new word. We called them Bombay movies. Of course, I knew about them because I grew up in Bombay and they were all around. I had various members of my family and family friends who did this or that in the Bombay movies, so I had a kind of insight into it. And like everybody else I went to those films. I thought of them as kind of enjoyable trash. There is a place in life for a hamburger, but you don't compare it to great cuisine. This was the junk food of India.

Yes, I took it seriously. It seems to me that there is a way in which you can compare the strategy of the Bombay movies to the strategy of the Elizabethan theater. You could actually compare Bollywood to Shakespeare. Take *Hamlet*. The first scene of *Hamlet* is a ghost story, the second scene is political intrigue at court, the third scene is a love story, the fourth scene is comedy with clowns and so on, and then you are back to the ghost story, then you're back to the political intrigue, then you're back to the love story. So you have four or five different kinds of stories, with only the genius of Shakespeare to hold them all together. I think one of the great freedoms that Shakespeare gave to the writers in English was that a story did not need to be one thing; it could be five things so long as you knew how to tell it. Bombay films do exactly that. Every movie is in part a melodrama, in part a comedy, in part a musical, in part a love story, all jumbled together with bad choreography and terrible songs, and wet sari sequences. Bombay cinema tells many different kinds of stories, trying to juggle them around and not to make it feel like a mess, but somehow make it seem whole. That is something that I thought I liked.

And I do like Indian classical music. Maybe I've got to write a novel about an Indian musician now. One of the things about Indian music that I really like, which is different from the Western classical tradition, is that the performer is also the creator of the work. In the Western tradition, the music is all written down and the performer performs it. There's an absolute split between composition and performance. Indian classical music is more like jazz: the ragas exist as a structure, but the space for improvisation and individuality inside the raga is great. The removal of the distinction between creation and performance, which happens in jazz, also happens in Indian classical music, and I respond very strongly to that.

There have been people who have not liked my books, who have said about them that they are too much of a performance. I take it as a compliment. You go down a certain path because it opens up before you, and you go down it to see where it is going, exactly as a musician will go down a certain improvisation. And at the end of it, you decide if you are going to keep it or not in the book. You can't keep all of those things, otherwise the book just goes off in tangents all the time. But it's wonderful to have that possibility—to allow something to just take hold of the text and to be able to improve and flow into it. In that sense, I think I have been affected by it, by Indian classical music.

NOTES

1. February 14, 2003.
2. See the chapter by Thomas Blom Hansen in this volume.

The Literary Rushdie

An Interview by Gauri Viswanathan

Salman Rushdie was interviewed about literature by Gauri Viswanathan, professor of English and Comparative literature, Columbia University. What follows is an edited version of that conversation. Rushdie read from two of his novels, The Moor's Last Sigh *and* Midnight's Children. *The interview begins after Rushdie's reading from* The Moor's Last Sigh.

Gauri Viswanathan: Thank you so much, Salman. I want to express my deep appreciation to the University Musical Society [of the University of Michigan] for inviting me. This is such a privileged occasion, and I'm absolutely delighted to have the opportunity to be in a conversation with Salman. A friend of mine once put *Midnight's Children* in my hand when it first appeared and told me, with great excitement and urgency, "You have to read this. It's about us." There was in her a sense of enthusiasm and excitement that finally there was a book that was speaking to us in a way that we hadn't quite had before. It was a very powerful moment in my consciousness of a new voice speaking to us.

First of all, in talking about the format of this conversation I want to take my cue from Salman, specifically something that he said yesterday in his conversation with Ashutosh Varshney. Ashu was asking about the influence, if any, of Indian classical music on Salman's art, and Salman responded by saying that if there is an influence, it is in terms of the improvisational character of the music that's reflected in his own writing, something akin to jazz. And I just want to say for the benefit of the audience that in a way what I'm going to do today will be a kind of improvisation. It will be the great rambling interview— very much like the great rambling Indian novel.

But I do want to come back to this point about the novel being about *us*. I've been thinking about who this "us" constitutes. There is a remarkable sense that Salman is speaking to a new generation of Indians, quite literally, you know, *"midnight's children,"* those who came into existence at the moment of India's independence. But that moment also inaugurates a new sense that there's a freedom to write, a freedom to think. And I was very much struck by a sentence in *Midnight's Children* where Salman writes that midnight's children—that is, the actual children, not the novel—midnight's children can either be the myth that modernization destroys or the voice of freedom, but they can't be construed as disease. And I think it is this inescapable quality of the midnight's children—those who are there, whose reality and existence must be acknowledged—that struck me so powerfully when I read the novel. And so I would like to begin by asking Salman: Who were you actually writing for? Who were you thinking of? Earlier on in your reading this evening you mentioned that there are struggles between fathers and sons, and sometimes that struggle between father and son takes the form of rebellion against the traditions that the father represents. While you were writing *Midnight's Children,* did you think of the novel as in fact a rebellion against an earlier tradition of writing, and that what you were producing was in fact the voice of the new son?

Salman Rushdie: I think yes, to an extent, that I did. Also frankly rebellion against my own father. When I told my father I wanted to be a writer, he said, "What will I tell my friends?" So I guess after *Midnight's Children* he sort of knew what to tell his friends, but that took a long time. First of all, I had to really prove to him and to myself that this business of becoming a writer was worth doing. And after an unsuccessful first novel, *Grimus,* which makes me hide behind the sofa when somebody starts reading it, it took me a very long time to find my way as a writer, and really the gamble that I took with *Midnight's Children* after the failure of the first novel was to do the most difficult, most ambitious, most risky thing that I could find to do, and it turned out to be this book. And yes, I did feel that what existed, certainly in English at that time, good as much of it was, didn't speak to me about the world that I knew and the world that I grew up in. One can read the novels of R. K. Narayan and one can admire them greatly, as I do. But the India they describe, which is largely rural or consists of very small towns in India, was not mine. And also the manner of the novels was very calm, mild, classicist, linguistically orthodox, and I just thought India is not like that. India is not calm and mild and classicist and linguistically orthodox. India is turbulent and noisy and vulgar and crowded and unorthodox, and you know it's a racket, and it's a sensual assault, and it's all these things. And I thought, "How can I do that?" and I guess the biggest initial question was to say the most obvious fact about India, that it's a crowd, it is a lot of people. How do you tell the story of a crowd? How do you tell the story of a multitude? The form of the novel emerged somewhat in response to that question that I asked myself. How do you tell a crowd of stories? How do you tell a story in which the central narrative certainly must exist and must be strong but, in a way, has to push its way through a crowd of other stories, bumps into stories in the streets, steps over them because they're sleeping on the sidewalk, whatever.

And I didn't find that sense in the books that were available to read. Although I admired many of them, especially Anita Desai's novels, Raja Rao's *Kanthapura*, G. V. Desani's *All about H. Hatterr*. Desani's novel is probably one attempt to be zany in the way I was hoping to be. But Desani often forgets to tell a story because he is so interested in the actual language games. I enjoyed the language games, but I got somewhat irritated by the fact that the story disappeared in long stretches in *All about H. Hatterr*. [Even books I admired] didn't feel to me like the place that I know. It's as simple as that, and since I couldn't find it, I tried to write it. I think I would never have dared to believe that the response to the book was what in fact took place, that so many people [responded in the way they did] . . . As you say, it's about *us*. And so many people felt described by it and expressed by it. It's a great, moving, humbling experience for a writer when a book becomes useful to people in that way. Writers on the whole—whatever they may pretend—on the whole are not that modest, and secretly every writer believes that the bracketing of Shakespeare is not such a big deal. He was good in his time. A little hard to read. He didn't write novels. So of course you kind of have the fantasy that your book is going to go out there and wow the world. But you don't really believe it. You know it to be a fantasy even while you are quite often energized by the dream because it helps you to keep going. . . . But when it turns out to be actually the case, it's kind of overwhelming. And what happened with *Midnight's Children* . . . I was very young. When I started writing the book, I guess I was twenty-seven, and when I finished writing the book, I was thirty-two. So it's a long, long time ago. And I was completely unprepared for the scale of the response to it. It was a good moment, and I think since then, as you say, there's been a great opening of the floodgates of Indian writing in English. There are many more writers now in a way that there weren't then. If I were now thinking about it, I wouldn't have that feeling of having to define myself against a previous literature, because now I think there's a very diverse literature. But at that time there just wasn't.

GV: What is so fascinating are the different kinds of experimentations that you did with the language, of course with English. Those experimentations are really striking given that you really couldn't be particularly sure where they were going, what kind of effects they would have. I think [for example, of] what seems to be a deliberate refusal to translate, to make easily available. You require the reader to work hard to figure out what things mean. And here I mean not an Indian audience but a Western audience.

SR: Yes. I just thought the hell with it. I had been very influenced and affected in my life by the great postwar novels of American writers, Jewish writers, like Philip Roth and Saul Bellow and Bernard Malamud and so on. You read Philip Roth and there's Yiddish everywhere and it's not translated. And if you're reading it from outside New York and you come across a word like *kishkes,* as in, "He gave him a zets in the kishkes," you have to work out from context that some kind of blow is being referred to and where. You don't exactly know where the *kishkes* are. Or what sort of blows *zetses* are like. You can see it hurts, and that's kind of enough. So I thought if these writers could do it, I could do it. And obviously you have to make it clear from context if the Hindi or Urdu word you're using is a swear word, or it's a kind of food, or whatever it might be. It has to be clear, but beyond that I thought: [let the reader] deal with it.

GV: Do you feel that sometimes that kind of experimentation could also lead to turning characters into almost stereotypical figures . . . well, let me backtrack a little bit: take Aurora [in *The Moor's Last Sigh*], for example. There are times when she uses words like *crackerfy, dirtify,* where she combines an Indian expression with an English word. Do you feel that at times using such repetitive utterances on her part may in fact reduce her to a stereotype of a certain class of person in India?

SR: I know a lot of people who speak like that, so I didn't make it up, I just heard it. So I think it's a question of using it. If it was just artificial, or invented, then it would seem arch. But I knew people who talked like that. In the end it's just the way she talks. The question of her character is a different question. I think she's one of my favorite characters, and I would certainly defend her against the charge of stereotype. After all, the stereotype of the Indian woman is somebody who is very mild and recessive and self-effacing, and Aurora is the opposite of that. She's very noisy, sexually predatory, aggressive, and she's a brilliant painter, and she's determined to put her art above the considerations of a private life and so on. She's like me, really.

GV: One of the episodes which I loved in the novel was one when [Aurora's son] goes to the school. The kindergarten and the teachers refuse to take the child, and Aurora takes them on in her own colorful way. . . . In fact, that was one of those instances where she does turn the language into another kind of [thing] . . . She appropriates not just the language but its idiomatic uses—for example, using the first name rather than talking about "Einstein" in a more recognizable fashion.[1]

SR: I don't think about it theoretically. That's the problem. When I was making up Aurora and found how she spoke, I enjoyed how she spoke. It's also a family trait. You know what happens in all families—not just Indian families—is that families have their own ways of saying things. Families [have] jokes and verbal tics; it's not at all unusual. So it's not just she who thinks like that, but it's the women who came before her who had the same kind of verbal tic. It's really a mark of dynasty, if you like. That little language goes down through the generations. Beyond that, when she starts talking, she is just talking. I'm really not thinking about theoretical considerations; I'm just trying to make the speech interesting, and I like the idea that her speech can be simultaneously funny and angry. She's genuinely outrageous and [consumed with] childhood intrigues and so on, but also funny. Speech can be both things at the same time. And I think that just gives it an extra quality, if you can make two things at once. So for me it was that: it was a way of allowing the manner of what was said to be slightly at odds with the content of what was said and as a result to give more depth to what was being said. In the end it's all instinct, it really is. It's mostly not done by rational thought. It's just done by ear and just what happens on the page and trying to judge whether that's good or not.

GV: Let's go back to the very interesting point that you made about having precursors in Jewish writers and the use of Yiddish. If Yiddish words could be used in ways that have a certain sort of cultural work attached to them, this would give you a lot more flexibility in the use of language. One thing that is so evident in your work is the fact that you are dealing with two different audiences: an audience that is very much in the cultural know and an audience that is outside that cultural sphere. So as you suggested, there are certain clues that you provide, yet at the same time you do make your readers work to gain access to the culture rather than to translate the culture and make it easily available. So the double perspective in your work is what I have often found one of the most exciting things that any writer, writing in English, has at his or her disposal—and yet at the same time probably the most difficult because you are aiming at two rather different audiences. The task as an artist would be, I think, to provide a coherence to your artistic goal and yet at the same time speak simultaneously to two different audiences.

Let me provide a context for the point that I would like to develop here. Yesterday in your conversation with Ashu Varshney you made a very powerful remark about how the England you portrayed fifteen or twenty years ago rendered Third World migrants as invisible, but that's certainly not the case today. There has been a great shift in the visibility of the South Asian immigrant populations in England through the interventions of work such as yours—work in literature, film, music, et cetera. . . .

As you also mentioned yesterday, *Midnight's Children* was probably the first novel to capture the Western imagination without itself being a novel about the Western experience of India. So your achievement is that you indeed did give visibility and voice to what had earlier been ignored, and you opened up a postcolonial critique of Britain's relations with its Asian minority communities. But it is equally clear that your novels just as passionately register a disappointment with the promise of postcolonial South Asia because of the rise of religious fundamentalism, and also the inevitable corruption at all levels of government and the state. So you have a critique of Britain's relations with its migrant communities, and at the same time you also have a critique of developments within South Asia. How do you keep these two different kinds of critiques working together, so that one does not overtake the other? Do you seek to invite readers to consider that the responsibility of people in England to minority communities there implies a similar responsibility which majority communities have to minorities in India?

SR: Yes, I guess so. Again the problem is that one can talk about [these interpretive matters and moral questions] after one has written a book. In the act of writing [such matters are indeed] partly what's in your head, but more so are questions of character, form, and language. [This is also true for] the question of the double audience. I think it needs to be talked about because it's true that the way these books have been read in India is rather different from the way they are read outside of India. When *Midnight's Children* came out, it had a wonderful reception everywhere. But the reception in the West tended to stress or highlight the more fantastical element of the novel, the more fabulous, surrealistic aspects of the novel, whereas in India it tended to be read more like a history book. And the fantasy elements were seen as being secondary to the portrait of preindependence and postindependence India.

Now in a way both readings are right. It's neither a history book nor is it a fairy tale. It's a history book disguised as a fairy tale, or a fairy tale disguised as a history book—I'm not sure which. But it was clear that people who deeply knew and felt connections to India were getting something from it, whereas the people who weren't in that position couldn't. But then I thought that's always true for books from anywhere really. When I first started reading Russian literature, my knowledge of Russia was not that great. I had never been there. I didn't speak Russian. I read in translation. And clearly someone who knew the world being described would find something in those books by Dostoevsky or Tolstoy that I might miss. I remember German-speaking friends talking about *The Tin Drum* by Günter Grass, which was a novel I really admired and was greatly affected by, one of the things that was completely lost in translation in *The Tin Drum* is that Grass tried very hard to re-create and memorialize a particular dialect of German, which was the dialect spoken in the villages at the German-Polish border in the north, where he grew up. And a lot of the dialogue of *The Tim Drum* is written in that dialect. And that had been an important part of his creative process, and somebody who reads only the translation can't capture it. When I started reading Latin American literature, for example, works by Borges and Marquez, I had never been to Latin America at that point. And again people would say about Gabriel García Márquez, if you know the history of South America, all kinds of things in *One Hundred Years of Solitude* become plain which otherwise seem like fairy tales; they actually describe real events. In the end my answer to that was, so what. I'm still reading a book that I'm enjoying. It may well be that there are nuances that I'm not getting. But there's plenty that I am getting, and that will do. And I guess that's what I think about my stuff, really. It's true that if people know about India, there are certain nuances that they will hear. But I hope that there's plenty that people will get anyway.

In the end I don't think about the reader. This is a terrible, truthful, horrible admission. I don't care.

GV: Do you really mean that?

SR: The terrible thing is yes. I never expected to be a best-selling writer. I really never expected that hundreds of thousands of people would go out and buy my books. My process as a writer is to be the servant of the idea, to try and make it work as best I can in all its dimensions, its character, story, language, form. And that frankly is the most difficult thing I've ever found to do. And when I'm doing it, I don't have time to think about how people will respond to it. I guess there is a kind of second me standing over my shoulder trying to see if I like what I'm doing, but frankly I don't know what people are going to like and what they're not going to like. And I rather dislike books that seem to be crowd-pleasing, that seem to be trying to go out there and pander to the imagined reader. I think readers will make up their own minds if the book has anything for them or not. That's for them to do. And I just think this is the gamble of literature, that you sit in your room and you do something as best you can. And having made it, you offer it out to the world, and if the world isn't interested, it's nobody's fault but your own. And if it is interested, then hurray for that. But it's not something you can really work towards. Unless you're trying to write a deliberate kind of popular fiction, an airport novel, for instance. There is such a thing as popular fiction which relies on certain machinery, simplifications of character, plot formula, and so on. It's the equivalent of a Bollywood movie. You can do that. I'm not interested in doing that. I'm interested in writing the stuff that represents to me a way of having a conversation about my relationship with the world I'm in. And making sense of that is the thing that takes all my time. After that, I hope people like it.

GV: I hope I can say something banal here. I take your point that you're not really thinking in terms of an audience as you are writing and that there is almost an intuitive process by which your novels are produced and that perhaps your real audience is that other self you are in conversation with. Yet at the same time you have made certain choices as a writer to write in a certain language and to also publish in certain places as well. So given those choices of language as well as publication, it does become inescapable to think of the reader. Otherwise you might be writing in another language altogether.

SR: Truthfully, I didn't have a language choice. By the time I got to the age where I was going to be writing books, it was quite clear that if I was going to write anything, it would be in English. If I write letters to my mother in Hindi or Urdu she very rapidly tells me how bad my Urdu is. Yes, I can speak Urdu and Hindi, but I wouldn't dream of writing in these languages, because frankly my command isn't good enough. So in the end the language chose me; it wasn't I that chose it. Having said that, yes, it was very important to me when I wrote *Mid-*

night's Children that people in India should respond well to it. And that's to say it would have felt to me that there was something wrong with the book had this not been the case. Because, as you were mentioning earlier, my worry was that [so much writing about India in English] had to do with Western experiences in India, and I didn't want this novel to feel like another outsider novel. I wanted it to be an insider novel. I wanted people to say, it's about us.

GV: But then you are thinking of the reader?

SR: Yes, I was, I confess, at that point. But the reader I was still thinking of was me. I was trying to write the book that I couldn't find to read, because that book, I felt, would describe, or should describe, the world that I grew up in. Of course I hoped that other people who grew up in that world would feel the same way, but my only antennae, my only guiding light, my only tuning fork was what I already knew about that world. And certainly I felt that if the book had been rejected in India, I would have been very depressed. The way in which the book was seized upon in India . . . it's wonderful when your book does well. I'm not saying I'm not interested in readers. But I'm saying, I'm only interested in readers after I finish the book. Because during the writing of it, it's too tough. No, let me be more accurate than this. The really difficult thing is to make something out of nothing. That's the slow, extremely problematic business of just putting [words] on the page for the first time. It takes much longer than subsequent drafts do, and it really can be very hard. So at that time all you can think of is trying to make sense of the idea that you've got. Once it's there on the page in however crude a form, however wrong it is, once there's something on the page, then it's true that a second intelligence kicks in. The second intelligence is more critical, where you have to be your own critic, and where you do begin to think about how the pages read. And you do want to make sure that it reads well. So the truth is somewhere in between the two positions. The first, difficult phase of creation is entirely about *it* and not about anything outside. But then the equally important second phase where you shape it, revise it, critique it, cut it, change it, hopefully make it better, is something where you are considering that, well, this is a page somebody else will read. And you want to make sure that it's a page that has all kinds of things that will be enjoyable to read. One of the good things about having at an early age acquired a lot of readers—many of whom have stayed along for the ride—is that you really don't know who they are because they're too many kinds of people. And readers bring to it everything that they have. They come from so many different backgrounds that I wouldn't know how to write for them. All I can think of is, if they like that, they may just want to see what I want to do next. And sometimes they do and sometimes they don't.

GV: This is a very important issue which connects with yesterday's conversation about the writer's responsibility to his or her reading public, and I'm really glad that you raised this point about so many multiple readerships, that it's really quite unclear what a reader will do with any work you have written. And looking at your own work, what is fascinating is that you span both colonial history as well as postcolonial history. So at one level *Midnight's Children* and *The Moor's Last Sigh,* for example can be critiques of colonial legacy, while at another they can be read as critiques of the failure of postcolonial promise.

SR: Yes.

GV: When you read these works in India or in South Asia, as a whole one can engage in the critique of the failures caused by corruption, fundamentalism, violence, et cetera in a way that is very meaningful, and one is absolutely grateful that there are critical voices that continue to keep leaders on their toes—because such voices are an important aspect of contemporary Indian life. Yet at the same time—and here I'm just raising this very hypothetically to you—is there also the possibility that readers who are outside the South Asia ambit might look at those depictions of failure and say, Aha! this points to exactly the fear that the departing colonizers had that once you leave India, then it will be total chaos?

SR: Maybe. Maybe. People say all kinds of stupid things. But my view is that it's just for me to respond to the world. And I think the danger of what you're saying is that one should only create positive images. And that would be . . . nobody would be sitting here.

GV: Actually, that's really not what I'm saying because it's not about positive images. To give an example, I have often seen when we talk about violence in Gujarat or the rising Hindu fundamentalist militancy, when we talk about that over here in the United States, people who call themselves very concerned Hindus tell me: Why are you washing dirty linen in public? You shouldn't talk about these things out here, you should only talk about that in India. And of course my response is exactly that these issues are not confined just to India and must be discussed . . . I'm not suggesting that at all.

SR: My view is you can talk about everything everywhere. That's to say, going back to politics, we can talk about the violence and arrogance of a lot of Western cultures. Violence is not the unique property of the East, as you can judge by that bomb that was exploded in Florida yesterday.[2] But I think there is this stuff to say: *The Moor's Last Sigh* is a novel that comes out of my experience of India as an adult, whereas in a way the inspiration of *Midnight's Children* was from my experience of India as a child. *The Moor's Last Sigh* is, underneath the surface, a much darker novel than *Midnight's Children;* it has much more to do with the kinds of failures that you talk about. But the surface of it is very bright. And I think the point that the book tries to make is that both things are true. Both the brightness, the vibrancy, the life, the incredible passion of the world being described, and the underlying corruptions and so on—both things are true. I'm not trying to say one thing or another, because otherwise it would just be a narrow polemic. The kind of vision of the world, I hope, in all my books is not one-dimensionally critical. But I am by nature satirical, and a satirist needs to be sharp. There's no point in a satire which is not sharp; it doesn't get anywhere. For example, in *The Moor's Last Sigh,* the character of the fascistic Hindu politician was seen by some people—goodness knows why—to be a version of the fascistic Hindu politician that actually exists in Bombay, Bal Thackeray. It may be by the purest coincidence that Bal Thackeray started his life as a political cartoonist and so does the character in my book.

GV: And has the name of an English author.

SR: Yes, that's right, he's called Fielding instead of Thackeray. But apart from these things, of course, they're completely unrelated. Well, actually they are. Let's just say they're politically connected, but they're not so like each other as people. In fact, my character is more lovable than Bal Thackeray. I tell you parenthetically in 1987 at the fortieth anniversary of the independence of India I went to India and made a documentary film, a state-of-the-nation film where instead of talking to politicians we just talked to ordinary people. We talked to the generation of midnight's children, that is, people born in 1947. And some people who were also forty in 1987. And one of the people who we interviewed was in fact one of the politicians from the Shiv Sena, the fascistic party that had sometimes taken control of Bombay. And he had been the first Shiv Sena mayor of Bombay and he was stunning. He was overtly racist and fascist in a way that wouldn't have been heard in Europe since the end of Nazism, really. On his desk in his office he had a telephone in the shape of a green plastic frog and every time the phone rang it croaked. And he would pick it up and have this frog against his face and he would be talking this horrendous stuff into this frog. So though we filmed it, in the end we didn't use it in the documentary because it made him lovable. You can't really hate somebody who is talking to a frog. But in the *Moor* I put the green plastic frog back in because it's too good. Yes, I called him by the name of the frog, "Medak" in Hindi. But this is the thing, you see, real life is much more interesting than anything you can make up. All you have to do is look at it and you see a fascist talking to frogs.

GV: I still would like to push you on this point about the two audiences. In *The Satanic Verses* you bring out so poignantly the plight of South Asian immigrants in Britain. Looking at the way you represent the relationship of Hindu communities to Muslim communities in South Asia—at least in the Bombay of *The Moor's Last Sigh,* where this is so vividly portrayed—I have been struck by how, putting these two contexts together, we might conceive the relationship of majority communities to minorities. This is a very powerful aspect of your works, which can be read in parallel ways in these two books about these two sites.

SR: I think that's right. You mentioned *The Satonic Verses* . . . clearly that was an example of what happens when people read the book in a certain way—or don't read the book in a certain way. But also the thing I've been saying is every writer wants in a way not to prescribe the reading of the book. You want to let the book go out and let readers complete the book. You want people to bring whatever it is they have in themselves and add that to whatever it is the book has and make that composite book. That's the joy of reading—it's different for every reader. So as a writer, I certainly—and most writers I know—really dislike trying to say, here's what the book's about and this is how you should think about it or how you should read it. But clearly what can happen, and what happened in that case, was that people made what I would call a radical misreading of the book. And yet, of course, my other self says they've got a right to read it any way they choose. And if that's what they get from it, then oops! But of course the problem was that the reading was highly politicized and affected by input from politicians and priests and so on. It was a big problem to know what you do with the text when people's readings of it diverged so violently. And that became for me a much more serious question than a lot of the other questions that got more airtime, the question of whether somebody should be killed [on the basis of a particular reading] is not a simple one to make a decision about—especially if it happens to be you! And my view is that I was against it. But these questions are much deeper and more problematic questions. What happens when people, in my view, misread the text, but in their view they weren't misreading the text? In their view, they were reading the text in a way that made them dislike it intensely. And then I was forced into the position which is exactly the position that I've always tried not to get into, which is to have to explicate the novel, to sit there and explain it. And fourteen years later I'm still doing it.

At least now I think I'm more able to shut up about it, because the great thing about the fuss having died down is that finally the book is beginning to have a moment which it never had when it came out, a moment of being read as a book and studied. Of course the echo of the trouble is still there and probably will be there for awhile, but it's beginning to become a footnote rather than the main thing. And so it's finally getting a reading. And what you discover is people like it or don't like it. Or they like it a bit, don't like it a bit. Finally *The Satanic Verses* is having the ordinary life of a book.

GV: How do you respond to the fact that some of the [initial] readers of *The Satanic Verses* may not necessarily have been speaking from a mosque or critiquing the work from the perspective of religious orthodoxy, but in fact were responding to the work as Muslim immigrants in Britain who saw a certain representation of Islam as in fact encouraging—perhaps entirely beyond your control—but none the less, encouraging a certain attitude amongst white Britons.

SR: Yes, but I defy you to find those passages in the novel. I challenge you. I will give you a million dollars if you can find those passages in the novel.

GV: Actually I just want to complete my thought . . . What many of them did say wasn't simply about disputing the truthfulness or fidelity of the text, but in fact they were referring to their sentiments: the sentiments of a minority group that had been aggrieved. And this had less to do with points of orthodoxy than with their relationship to white Britain. That it is what they feared had been jeopardized [by your book] . . .

SR: The novel is in fact a portrait of their relationship with white Britain. The novel is about immigrants to England from the Indian subcontinent, and many of those immigrants in the novel are of Muslim backgrounds, not all of them. I think anybody who reads the novel can see that the lives of those people are portrayed extremely sympathetically. It's an attempt to enter into what was then an invisible reality to try and make it visible. I know there is nothing in *The Satanic Verses* that is a study of Islam or a version of Islam. In *The Satanic Verses* the prophet is not called Muhammad and the city is not called Mecca. The religion is not called Islam, which in my view allows it to be considered as fiction. But apparently that didn't work. And one of the reasons I did that is because I was trying to say that the subject here is not only Islam. But the question of revelation is really the subject being discussed there, and I'm using a version of Islam because I know most about it. But it could apply equally to other revelations.

There is nothing there that I first of all haven't heard people sit around in rooms and talk about in much the same language. There is a lot in there that can be justified by looking at the traditions of the prophets. A great deal of what is written there about the nature of the revelation that came to the prophet Mohammed is taken more or less directly from preexisting texts in the Hadith traditions of the prophet. For example, when he is shown in the novel as having various encounters with the revelation, he says . . . "Well the real prophet said that he didn't always see things, he sometimes only heard things. Sometimes they were unclear." The prophet said sometimes it seemed like the thing that he was getting was emerging from within him. That he felt often a great pain in his stomach. That something was being extruded. He says that often the pain would be so intense that he would fall down and roll around and had many of the characteristics of epileptic seizure. And if you compare—this is not me, this is him, although there is a version of that in the book—if you compare that to the accounts of revelation that exist in other religious traditions, Joan of Arc and St. John the Divine, whatever it might be, they're incredibly similar. So what I was interested in is a phenomenon that is clearly transcultural.

The phenomena of revelation and the mystical experience are interesting to study even if you ask yourself the question, if you had been standing on the mountain next to the Prophet, would you have seen the archangel? And my answer to that question would be probably no. At the same time it's clear that what is happening to him is entirely a sincere and genuine experience, so the question then is, what does it mean that he is seeing something that I would not see if I stood next to him. And that's one of the things I was trying to explore.

Actually I thought the whole Islam bit in *The Satanic Verses* was a serious inquiry of that sort. But from the point of view of somebody who is not a believer, it got turned into a very crude caricature of itself. For example, mosques in England would send around xerox sheets in which little lines of dialogue from the novel were taken out and presented as my view. So, for instance, there are scenes in the novel in which the early religion is being persecuted and early members of the religion are being verbally and physically abused by the mob in the city not called Mecca. And some of that abuse is there. And some of those sentences were taken out and presented as my abusive view of Islam.

If you're going to make a portrayal of the attacks on a newborn faith, how can you do it without showing the attackers doing the attacking? If those attacks are then made into your view, it's a distortion. And some of the trouble came from that kind of distortion. But I do think, and I always thought, that there are people of orthodox religious belief who are not going to like this book because it has an unorthodox view of religion, and it seemed to me that was all right—you go ahead and read another book!

GV: I'm glad you concluded this remark with references to religion, because this really connects to my last question before we have your reading from *Midnight's Children*. You alluded earlier to magic realism. For a long time I've felt that to put you in a tradition aligning you with Gabriel García Márquez is not really doing justice to what I think is actually a far richer texture to your work—a texture which may have different genealogies. Here I'm speaking to some extent of my own personal interests and areas of study. I've been very struck by how there is a running strain of invisibility in your novels—be it when you talk about the invisible workers in England or when you refer to the invisible laws of nature. You talk about invisible realities, phenomena beyond the visible, and in *The Moor's Last Sigh*, I was struck by your many references to Theosophy, to Annie Besant and Madame Blavatsky. I think in *Midnight's Children* you refer to telepathy as universal thought forms. And that's actually a phrase that is Annie Besant's. I wonder if there is any connection between your idea of magic—and I'm not using the word *magical* or *realism* here but rather magic and the occult and invisible laws of nature and the alternative religious formulations that acquired such currency around the time of the Indian independence movement, as you point out in *The Moor's Last Sigh*.

SR: It's really a great question. As an individual in the world, I'm not at all religious. As a person writing about the world that I came from, it is absolutely impossible to leave the religious dimension out because you're just not describing the world if you do. This is a world in which many gods are very healthily alive and believed to be directly acting on the daily lives of people. So you have to make that an aspect of your work. And what it does is that it gives me as a writer—I dislike so much the word *spiritual* because I think it sounds like something from California these days—I think it should be outlawed for fifty years until we find out what it means again. Anybody who goes into his imagination for a living is aware that there is a thing in human beings which is not flesh and blood. There is a place that you [go to when you write], out of which stuff comes, and you don't know where it comes from, and it sometimes feels to be unreal outside yourself and coming through you and so on, which is no doubt an illusion because it's not coming from anywhere else. I make it up.

But you have that sense of another dimension. You have to because that's what the imagination opens to you—it opens other dimensions to you. And so that has led me to try and find ways of allowing the sense of those other dimensions to come into the writing in a way that you very accurately just mentioned. And I've read a lot of that stuff, Theosophy, Krishnamurthi, and all that stuff, but I don't particularly go for it. But it's sometimes a useful way in the realistic course of a novel set at a certain place, at a certain time, to try and open what one might have to call the "doors of perception."

I discovered, by the way—and this is a completely bathetic end to the story—in Los Angeles on the corner of Beverly Boulevard and La Cienega Boulevard there is a pharmacy called Rexall, which should be visited by everyone who loves literature because it is in this pharmacy that Aldous Huxley for the first time tried mescaline. And actually the doors into this pharmacy are in fact the doors of perception. These are the places that don't often get onto the literary tours. But once you've learned Huxley had his first trip there, you can't think of it just as a pharmacy anymore. So in that sense I think yes, writing is about opening the doors of perception.

There's a thing that I've always carried around with me which I will just say as the last thing before I stop. Saul Bellow has a character in his novel *The Dean's December* who hears in the distance the barking of a dog—insistent, unstopping barking of a dog. And because it's a dog in a Bellow novel, the character imagines that the dog's barking is a protest against the limitations of dog experience. And he imagines what the dog is saying in his barking is, "For God's sake open the universe a little more." A beautiful Bellow sentence. No other writer could have written such a great sentence. And I've often thought, that's the job. That's the job. Open the universe a little more.

GV: Thank you, Salman.

NOTES

1. The allusion is to this passage in *The Moor's Last Sigh:* "My mother was incensed. 'Who-all have you got in class?' she demanded. 'Einsteins, is it? Little Alberts and Albertinas, must be? A whole school-ful of emcee-squares?'"

2. A reference to the MOAB bomb, tested at Eglin Air Force Base, Florida, on March 11, 2003. At the time it was the most powerful nonnuclear bomb ever detonated.

Essays on Salman Rushdie ☙

AKEEL BILGRAMI

Twenty Years of Controversy

Philip Roth once said about the literature of Eastern and Western Europe that in totalitarian regimes, "Everything matters, so nothing goes," while in modern liberal democracies in the West, "Nothing matters, so anything goes."[1] That, if it is true, cannot, of course, be literally or perfectly true; but even as an approximation, it registers a familiar distinction often reflected in discussions of liberal democracy and its various "Others." The distinction is particularly worth exploring in the context of a novel like *The Satanic Verses*,[2] written *from* a world that has routinely come to be perceived by its critics as falling within the caption "Nothing matters, so anything goes," and which (at least partly) is *about* a world (the world as conceived by so-called Islamic fundamentalism) that its author claims, at length and with brilliant irreverence, to fall within the contrasting slogan "Everything matters, so nothing goes."

Roth expresses things slightly misleadingly in his formulation of this latter ideal. He must surely have had in mind to say, "Only one thing matters, so nothing else goes." But the misformulation is understandable on the assumption that if only one thing matters, it is taken to be everything, so that other things are not so much as visible on the horizon. The idea then must be that when other things surface and intrude on the horizon to present conflict, they are, by these monolithic lights, intolerable.

I am pressing on with this abstract caricature in Roth to bring into focus an image not of Islamic fundamentalism but of Islam itself, an image familiarly presented in semiliterate Western imaginings, and equally familiarly repudiated by a recent intellectual tradition of ethnography as well as of literary and philosophical criticism. My subject in this essay is the perception of Rushdie's novel in the context of this image *and* its repudiation because it seems to me that something important gets lost or, at any rate, cramped in such ideological disputation.

In earlier writing on Rushdie and on Islam,[3] I had tried to subvert the distinction Roth appeals to from two different directions.

On the one hand by arguing that the liberal ideal, as it is expressed in the slogan, quite apart from the exaggeration, fails to describe liberal doctrine accurately because the idea of "anything goes" is sanctioned only if one erects the concept of tolerance and of the First freedom as the *one thing* that matters above all. On this conception of modern liberal society, the slogan cannot any longer read, "Nothing matters, so anything goes," but rather, "Only because one very specific thing matters above all else does anything go." Such an understanding of liberalism is often criticized by those who argue that "you can't just say anything; free speech is not without limit or constraint." John Le Carré's criticism of Rushdie, for instance, took this form.[4] But that is hardly the interesting question raised by Rushdie's book, and it is only if one understands liberal commitments in this simplistic way that such a simplistic form of criticism could surface as the relevant objection. Perhaps some will be inclined to such an understanding of liberalism, but I had argued that the more subtle and difficult problem with standard versions of liberalism lay elsewhere. It lies in the fact that so much of classical liberal doctrine, which still dominates modern thought and practice, has taken the form of a priori philosophical argument in favor of liberal principles of tolerance. By "a priori," I mean something very specific, I mean an argument that appeals to no substantive value commitments of citizens. So, for instance, Mill argued that principles regarding freedom of speech are derivable from roughly the following argument. "Our opinions have been wrong in the past. That is evidence that our present opinions may be wrong. Therefore, we should tolerate dissent from our present opinions, just in case they are wrong." Such an argument is a priori in the sense that it is supposed to appeal to *anyone capable of reason,* whatever they might value. Mill gave other arguments for free speech as well, much more modest ones, such as the argument that we should adopt free speech as a principle because it allows for diversity of opinion. This argument is more modest because it does not lay claim to being persuasive to anyone capable of reason, but only to those who value diversity. It rests therefore not with some universal conclusion about the rationality of free speech, but rather, because it appeals to a substantive value (the value of diversity), which some people may embrace and others may not, it rests with a conclusion about its reasonableness only for those who do embrace it.[5] I had defended Rushdie against the efforts of Muslims in many parts of the world to censor him, not by the first, ambitious form of argument, but rather the second, more modest form. I did so because I don't believe that there are *any* effective arguments for free speech (or indeed *any other* political or moral principle) that ought to be persuasive to anyone, so long as they are rational, independent of any substantive values they hold.

And from the other direction, I tried to undermine Roth's distinction by arguing that the moral-psychological economy of ordinary[6] Muslims was far more internally contradictory (even if only implicitly and latently so) than the distinction would acknowledge, and that the best case that can be made for Rushdie is to argue that *The Satanic Verses* critically addresses many of those aspects of religious doctrine that the large majority of ordinary, non-"fundamentalist" (though devout) Muslims were themselves implicitly repudiating in many of their de facto secular social formations and habits. He was, in short, their ally against fundamentalist conceptions of Islam, and it was inconsistent therefore to entirely dismiss him and his book in the way that most of these very Muslims had done. If a realization of this implicit internal inconsistency eventually brought, in its wake, an increasing commitment to principles of freedom of speech among Muslims, even in the context of Rushdie's blasphemous novel, that would not be because these principles were plonked down as some philosophically established universal truths of Millian liberal doctrine, but rather because they issued from the resolution of such internal tensions within Muslim values.

This form of internal criticism by Muslims had a much better chance of coming to a viable defense of Rushdie, I claimed, than the one that aspired to ulterior forms of universality and objectivity for liberal principles. But it was constantly blocked by a picture of the dispute that was to be found in the stark distinction that Roth's slogans described.[7] Internal criticism of laws of blasphemy from within Islam by appeal to other values that Muslims hold is only possible if Islamic populations are *conflicted*—conflicted between their commitment to a religion in which there are doctrinal elements regarding prohibition of blasphemy and their commitment to values that lend support to greater freedom of speech. In general, internal arguments can only be given when there is internal conflict of this kind. One set of values can then be deployed to give reasons to shed the other opposing value commitments. That is what is meant by "internal" criticism or deliberation deploying "internal" reasons. But if Roth's slogan is true of Islam (as he says it was of Eastern European nations) and only one thing matters, then presumably *there is no* internal conflict, and no scope for defending Rushdie against their religious commitments that would censor blasphemy.

What is much more surprising, however, is that The *Satanic Verses,* has been particularly difficult to defend along these internalist lines I had proposed, not because of such caricaturing slogans but because of a much more considered challenge coming from scholars and critics who are highly sympathetic and knowledgeable about Islam. I don't mean sympathies and challenges of a superficial sort that simply say, "Tolerance does not mean that you can say anything, however offensive," such as those voiced by John Le Carré. The really difficult and interesting issues are not addressed by such simply stated reactions to Rushdie, and for all my admiration and respect for Le Carré, I think Rushdie's irritable response to him was to some extent justified, given how crudely he had presented his objections.[8] What I have in mind when I say there is an especially difficult challenge that one has to meet if one is going to defend Rushdie is a criticism of him that goes something like this. (A good example of one of its proponents is the anthropologist Talal Asad.)[9]

First, some background. Before looking at the local Muslim response to Rushdie in Britain, which is Asad's main focus, it is worth recording the response at the global level, and the material and psychological condition of many of the nations with predominantly Muslim populations from which that response comes. In an interesting way the issues at the global and the more local level are structurally the same.

In the global picture nobody any longer really denies (except perhaps a writer such as Naipaul, who in his pursuit of surface cultural criticism of various Islamic peoples has cultivated a deliberate ignorance about both their histories and their political economies), the Muslim reaction is to a large extent a product of a certain attitude of resentment that has developed over years of colonial rule. Even after decolonization the West's corporate-driven undermining of the material lives of many Muslim populations today, its support for Israel against Palestinian aspirations for the most elementary of freedoms, the failure in the past of Arab nationalism to shake that support and generally to forge a sense of postcolonial autonomy and dignity, and the recent humiliation by the imperial invasions of Afghanistan and Iraq, have all contributed to a continuation of that attitude even among ordinary, nonfundamentalist Muslims. As a result the West's support for Rushdie, a novelist who is perceived as being offensively critical of Islam from the point of view of modernity and with the literary techniques of postmodernity, is bound to be seen as just another arrogant symptom of long-standing Western domination and postures of condescension and contempt.

This psychology at the global level among nations with predominantly Muslim populations is replayed at the local level among the immigrant Muslim minorities in European nations like Britain, where Rushdie lived and wrote, and this cannot be surprising because it is the product of very similar material relations. It should go without reminding but perhaps it will not, so I will remind you that the first large

(margin note, handwritten, left side:) Rushdie as symptom of western dominance + contempt

wave of Muslim immigration to Britain and other European nations was a result of the relative privileging of the metropolitan proletariat due to surpluses produced by a century of the international spread of Western capital by colonial rule, and also a result of the need to meet the labor shortage in European countries in the decade or more of reconstruction after the Second World War. This wave of immigration was the product of a deliberate policy decision by the governments of many European nations, and it led in subsequent decades to further immigration of families in a pattern that is now well known and well studied. Once again, therefore, as with colonial rule, and once again due to causes that emerge from the movement of the forces and demands of capital, nonwhite populations were brought together with Western populations, this time *in Western nations*. The inequalities first created by colonial rule at the global level were in fact now being echoed *within* the borders of Western nations themselves.

With this background of colonial history and postcolonial migrant formations in place, Asad's argument can be summarized as roughly this. Though these immigrants are granted various forms of political equality as the liberal state conceives of them, it is not allowed as a negotiable question, in the context of a "blasphemous" book, whether the First freedom is indeed first. In the global picture, this liberal position is presented as the culmination of hard-won historical progress in the Western world to which the lagging colonies and neocolonies must now also aspire to evolve. In the local migrant context in Western nations, the argument is more straightforward: the liberal perspective is simply, "This is how we are. These are our liberal values of free speech, and if you have come to live here, these are the laws you must learn to live under." The point is often extended, of course, to a far wider range of values than freedom of expression, to include such things as what is worn on one's body and head, what is taught in one's schools, what is paraded on the streets, and so on. Sometimes there is a concession to cultural autonomy in the exercise of such cultural values so long as it is restricted to a sphere in which the basic defining features of the liberal state are left untouched. That is the ideal of multi*culturalism* as we have come to know and love it. But as soon as the Muslim demands something that runs up against the *political* values of free speech upheld by the state, as happened in the aftermath of the publication of Rushdie's book, the limits of multiculturalism were immediately revealed. The British liberal state would not make any concessions.

Such a critique is a much harder and more sophisticated challenge to meet than the simplicities of Roth's distinction and Le Carré's heartfelt sympathies for Muslim sensitivities. How should one respond

free speech as a [illegible] value

to it, if one still wishes to defend Rushdie? Is there still some relevance to the general line of defense I had given of Rushdie in responding to this critique?

The first thing to notice is the way in which Asad's critique presents the matter as one of wholesale relativism. British society simply lays down the law: "This is how we are, these are our laws, so you better adapt to them if you are here." But the Muslims, who were allowed there by international immigration policies to fulfill British economic ends, and are now full and rightful citizens of the land, can with equal right claim their own alternative *nomic* structures, which in the context of a "blasphemous" book, will clash with liberal laws. That is the relativist impasse. It is law versus law. And multicultural accommodation is not to the point, or not the primary point. It is wrong of the state to insist on something that is genuinely disputable by its legal citizens. Granting those citizens superficial cultural concessions of headdress et cetera is not the accommodation that is needed. What is needed is an acknowledgment that there is an impasse here on fundamental values, and minority rights require that the Muslim demand for censorship is not dismissable by the liberal state.

Now, it was partly my point in those early writings that introducing relativism in this way into the dispute is not to introduce anything very precise or instructive. The positing of a relativist impasse between two nomic systems—one making free speech primary, the other prepared to place free speech second in the context of what everyone acknowledges is a book that writes of a community's most deep and cherished notions with satirical contempt[10]—is to land one within a framework for the dispute that impoverishes the theoretical possibilities.

A first step in revising the framework that Asad's sort of critique imposes is to ask what underlies the British state's attitude. The attitude, I think, is a statist assertion of what I had earlier described as the doctrinal refusal to look for "internal" arguments for free speech, arguments that might appeal to some of the substantive values of ordinary, nonfundamentalist Muslims. On such a view, the assumption is that British society has evolved into values that have a greater or more objective right on their side, and so with that right behind it, the state has no other option but to impose liberal laws. These laws alone have the right on their side. Asad denies them this right and instead asserts a relative (or relativist) right on each nomic side (the values of both the liberal state and the Muslim community).

When the formulation of the framework of the dispute is revised in this way, one can begin to find a way out. To begin with, notice a curious thing. *Both* sides in the dispute, when the dispute is formulated in these revised terms, make an assumption that is quite wrong. It is basically an assumption about the nature of reason in politics and morals. The assumption is that if one cannot get reasons that all rational people are going to accept, then one is not in the realm of reason or reasoning with one another at all and there is an impasse, with a relativist right now on each side. This reduces the options, a reduction that *both* sides to the dispute, *despite* their deep opposition to one another, *share,* because of their shared assumption that there is nothing by way of reasoning when reasons of a classical liberal sort are found wanting.

Yet there are theoretical resources by which one may resist this narrowing theoretical assumption that they both take for granted. What that shared assumption does not admit in the space of rationality is any position for what I have called "internal" reason. But there still is scope, if we allow for a notion of internal reasons, to finesse the dichotomy on offer, that is, this dichotomy: either reasons that establish the high-profile objectivity of the liberal principle of free speech or a concession that the principle is just one among others, with only a relativized truth on each side. Allowing internal reasons would still require the liberal position to resist the claim that Muslims have an equal right to their laws when it comes to a matter of such depth of belief and feeling, but it would equally require the liberal *not* to do so by simply declaring that this is because they have come to the more modern and advanced society and must therefore live according to its liberal laws. Asad's complaint is against the latter position taken by the liberal state, and the complaint is perfectly justified. But such justification as it has in no way sanctions his further claim that therefore the liberal must admit in the name of minority rights that his own liberal principle of free speech is only one among others (even others that contradict it) each of which has a right, a relativist right, on its side. Rather it behooves the liberal to look for values *within* the Muslim populations (that is what makes the reasoning internal) that might lead them to conclude, despite their depth of feeling about Islam, that free speech may after all be primary. There is nothing in Asad's critique that rules this theoretical and practical possibility out. In fact, it is not clear that there is anything that *can* rule the *possibility* out.[11]

I have written elsewhere[12] about what the scope and the difficulties are for making these possibilities a serious prospect, so I won't rehearse those points here. But I do want to note that once one sees things in this broader framework, it ought to become clearer why it is increasingly unfair to blame Rushdie's novel (as Rushdie's critics such as Michael Dummett who are sympathetic to Muslim immigrants have done)[13] for being the source and trigger of the hostile reaction in European nations against Muslims for their defensive and censorious response to it. That backlash can now be seen rather as having its real and original source *not* in a deliberately insensitive work of literature, *nor* in the rigidity of a "backward" religious population migrated into alien liberal terrain, but as emerging from a prior refusal on the classical *liberal* state's part to acknowledge that the migration of cultural difference into one's midst should have the effect of laying it open to internal argument, which the state must use its conceptual and other resources to provide. And on the other side, the problem is compounded because this refusal by the liberal state to see values as emerging in negotiable internalist outcomes (a refusal coming from a conviction that they express a universal, philosophically justified truth that allows the state one has adopted therefore to simply impose it with a sense of self-justification) produces just the defensiveness among Muslim immigrants that we recorded in the global picture of colonial rule, and which makes it impossible for them to see Rushdie as a partial ally, despite his perceived rhetorical excesses.

This diagnosis should help to deflect Asad's and Dummett's and Le Carré's understanding of *The Satanic Verses,* as the willfully destructive ethnography of a Western-minded liberal author, deaf to the voices of unequal nations of the world and unequal citizens within the Western world.

The diagnosis views the magnitude and vehemence of the Muslim response to Rushdie as deriving from the fact that much more than private faith has been perceived to be under attack, since Islam in many parts of the world is a religion that has a very high political profile. Many of its political aspirations, however, are also the source of considerable anguish for ordinary Muslims since they are sometimes exploited to foist upon Muslim societies policies (and even sometimes regimes) that ordinary Muslims find highly objectionable. Zia's Pakistan, Hekmatyar's Afghanistan, Khomeini's Iran were just some of the examples that were vivid in Rushdie's time of writing *The Satanic Verses.* There is repeated proof that such qualms pervade the thinking of ordinary Muslims. Democratic national elections in any of these countries, when they have occurred, have never yielded more than a fractional vote for the Islamist parties. In general ordinary people have never supported such parties, nor are they ever likely to, except where Islam has been suppressed, as in Algeria and perhaps now in Egypt. Even in places where an absolutist Islamic political organization like Hamas does have support among Muslims, that is not because of its absolutism but because it is the only organization that is working hard and with some effectiveness to provide basic services (medical, educational, communicative . . .) as well as minimal structures of civil society, for one of the most brutalized peoples in the world.

How might this distaste for absolutism among ordinary, usually devout, but nonfundamentalist Muslims be exploited to give an "internalist" defense of the author of a book that has given these very same Muslims such deep offense? By first asking them not to forget that Rushdie has shown great sympathy for their condition in his excoriating critique in the very same novel of Thatcherite England's attitudes and policies toward its immigrant populations. And then, having done that, urging them, despite their feelings of hurt, also now to direct their attention to Rushdie's own anguish, to his own scorn and detestation for the absolutist Islamist vision and to ask them to respond to what seems to be a challenge thrown down by those sections of the novel in which Islam is most obviously the subject: Can we any longer separate the tyrannies of social and political practice in which Islam is so often invoked in Iran, say, or in Afghanistan under the Taliban, without being more critical of *ourselves* and our uncritical susceptibility to such absolutist exploitation of our justified resentment of Western domination of our lands and people? To try to meet this challenge would be to take the novel more seriously than Asad or Dummett or Le Carré would have Muslims do; it would be to awaken to the novel's significance for one's own goals as ordinary nonfundamentalist Muslims, and not simply to dismiss it with the charge of being offensive. Even if the challenge was successfully answered, an honest effort to think it through could not proceed without acknowledging that Rushdie was, for all his differences with the devout commitments of ordinary Muslims, their supporter in a common and worthy agenda. With that acknowledgment crucially in place, a nonabsolutist Muslim reader, even if he found the self-consciously postmodern irreverence of the novel alien and offensive, even if she disagreed with Rushdie's wholesale skepticism about the revelation and about Muhammad's unfaltering monotheism, could nevertheless be in a better psychological position to see it as merely Rushdie's own individual mode of pursuit of that shared agenda. Now, the excesses (if that is how one viewed them) of an ally's rhetoric may still offend, but he could hardly any longer be convicted of treachery.

These efforts to put the novel and its author under a more sympathetic light than where his critics, whom I have mentioned, have placed him are of course fraught with the difficulties created by an attitude of defensiveness against the West that I have said is pervasive among Muslims today, despite their dislike for the fundamentalists in their own society.

However, Muslim defensiveness with regard to the West is a very nuanced thing. In thinking about it historically, one must distinguish between hostility and defensiveness. For centuries the relations between Christian Europe and its growing Islamic neighbor were defined by a hostility in matters of territory and doctrine, and were displayed in the violence of wars and in the most vilifying propaganda against the other. But there was a robustness in this exchange and there was a perverse form of respect for each other that was shown by more or less equal foes. There was a genuine appreciation of and instruction in the achievement of the other in the wide span of culture, science, philosophy, and literature. It was only with the rise of Western colonial domination that this health of hostility eroded into a feeling of defensiveness bred upon the loss of autonomy and upon colonial attitudes of superiority and condescension. These are the attitudes that I said continue today in revised forms for the reasons I mentioned earlier. I stress all this to point out that it is not the clash of civilizations that is in itself the issue. As I have just said, there were sustained clashes for a long period in the past where such attitudes were quite absent. It is only when there is *conquest passing itself off as a clash* that these sentiments surface, as they continue to do today. The fact that today (since decolonization, that is) these conquests do not always take the overt form of invasions (though clearly they have started doing so once again) but rather the form of corporate-driven foreign engagements as well embargoes and sanctions, should not conceal the manifest element of conquest, of materially unequal and exploitative engagement. It is the psychology issuing from these subtle or blatant forms of conquest that has blinded ordinary Muslims to the point and usefulness the novel might have for their own value commitments.

Their response to Rushdie has tended to be that he has not helped their case at all in the struggle against Islamic fundamentalism. It is often said that he has provoked rather than condemned the fundamentalist, that he has—at best—shown bad judgment by having failed to see the extremity of the feelings he was going to provoke, and—at worst—he saw it all clearly and deliberately sought the publicity it brought him.

But it can surely be replied on his behalf that the fundamentalists have been and will be provoked by much less than Rushdie serves up, so it may be overscrupulous to worry about provoking them. By focusing on the fundamentalist response, they are failing to explore the questions that Rushdie's novel and the aftermath of its publication pose for *their own* goals, for the goals of the vast majority of Muslims who are as opposed to the fundamentalist element in their societies as they are hurt by the novel. The deepest issue, then, is whether the answers that such Muslims will, on reflection, provide to these questions are compatible with their own condemnation of the novel. If not, there is a fundamental but implicit contradiction in their position, and it is a matter of enormous consequence that they become alive to it. To be hurt and offended by the novel is one thing, a natural thing, for a devout person, however moderate. But to take up these questions and answer them with reason and intelligence is quite another thing, for it does not permit the offence to breed a stultifying defensiveness. I am not suggesting that Muslims will or should agree with Rushdie in his wholesale religious scepticism or his ideas about how the religious impulse is better gratified in our world by art and literature than by orthodox religions. But to disagree and to criticize him amount to taking his novel seriously and therefore to rejecting the sort of condemnation of it one finds so widespread among Muslims. Such disagreement will require that they provide a detailed answer to the question: how can Muslim nations work to build a just and free society in the sort of legitimizing religious framework that even the nonabsolutists among them have adopted, without surrender to or constant threat from the fundamentalist elements?

Recent history has repeatedly shown that the progressive possibilities of a politicized Islam amount to a dangerous myth. Rushdie's *Shame* and *The Satanic Verses* have done much to make this evidence vivid. If his novels are remembered for having raised once again the possibility of such reformist consciousness among moderate Muslims, it is hard to see what his bad judgment is supposed to consist in. It is hard to see why the publicity he has sought is selfish. As far as I can see, it has—at hideous cost to himself—publicized the desperate need for a reformed, depoliticized Islam.[14] It would be an ungenerous people that focused only on the satirical and parodic "excesses" of an author who had raised questions of such deep and primary significance for them.

When we move the focus from those whom I have been calling "ordinary" Muslims to those critics of Rushdie who have grown up with the literature and culture of the West, it is much worse than a lack of generosity. It is a failure to grasp the claims that Rushdie has always made for the very idea of writing, and especially of the novel and its inherent potential for cultural and political criticism, a potential with which his Western critics should be perfectly familiar. One crucial element in these claims is to be found in the stance that Rushdie takes on the *mode* of political and cultural criticism, a stance that all of Rushdie's novels brilliantly exemplify, namely, that the novel's power to criticize existing hegemonies cannot be restricted to the mode of argument and counterargument; it must if necessary take in, in its criticism, the hegemonizing compromises of that mode itself. It must commit itself to providing a clash of modes and languages. No doubt this runs the risk of being perceived as creating excesses, but the stance has always claimed that anything less comprehensive in its polemical and critical intention and effect would only perpetuate the forms and pieties that frame the hegemonies in question.

This stance is not hard to discern in *The Satanic Verses* unless one is distracted by one's own defensiveness, as Muslims might be, but presumably his Western critics have no reason to be at all. Anybody who notices that a novelist is disrespectful, not merely to a religious prophet and his family with the play of proper names, but to everything else he touches in every novel he writes, must surely pause to wonder whether there is a considered point underlying this comprehensiveness, and whether the particular things that offend him might have flowed from a more general conviction of what the possibilities of a novel are in the author's own conception of his work.

Nor, obviously, is the stance Rushdie's invention. It is admittedly true that in the last several decades in the West, the target of this stance has always been the bourgeois hegemonies of a culture shaped by a seemingly decaying but, in fact, highly resilient capitalism. As Brecht advised Benjamin: "Start with 'the bad *new* things.'" So it might seem startling and injudicious that an Anglo-Indian novelist brings this stance to a target that his Western critics would have us consider a "bad *old* thing," pre-Enlightenment religiosity, something that the West itself has outgrown, but to be discussed and criticized where it does exist in a more appropriately solemn mode. Rushdie is very well aware of this and has all along resisted the idea of the unsuitability of his adopted mode of writing for his subjects. The question Edward Said once rightly posed—Why did Rushdie fall into this Orientalizing misrepresentation of Islam?[15]—therefore, has an answer. In making a "bad old thing" the target of a postmodern cultural critical stance, *The Satanic Verses* repudiated the historicist restriction of appropriate stances for appropriate targets; it repudiated the restriction as *itself* another Orientalist withholding of the creative possibilities of Islam for its own self-understanding and self-criticism.

Frederic Jameson has written of the appropriateness of pastiche rather than parody in the context of postmodernist culture.[16] Though I happen to find this restriction unconvincing (for reasons that I can't possibly elaborate here), that is not because I am committed to the strong *general* claim that periodicity imposes no constraints on the effectiveness of such modes and stances. If that were so, my concern in the next paragraph for a politicized humanism, fitting for the postmodern literary sensibility, would have no validity. My claim is weaker and more particular. Putting aside Jameson, I am only claiming of Rushdie's stance as I have described it, first that there is a tendency to see it as yielding Orientalizing distortions and excesses in the context of its particular target—Islam—because of a perceived inappropriateness of that stance for that target; and second this perception of inappropriateness, this restriction of what Islam may employ for its own self-criticism, smacks of the very Orientalism that it charges the stance of having fallen into. Why should well-known antecedents to Rushdie within this stance, such as, for example, the films of Buñuel and Arrabal (sickening to devout Christians), be any more justified in their intended power to undermine the seemingly perpetual conserving tendencies of bourgeois European culture than Rushdie's intentions in his own novel, to undermine the constricting and conserving dimensions of the holy for Islamic reform?

Literature and criticism, in the world in which Rushdie was educated and lived and wrote *The Satanic Verses,* has witnessed the passing of Leavisite humanism and modernism; and more recently it witnessed the inabilities of an avowedly antihumanist, structuralist, and poststructuralist ideology, which succeeded it, to cope with its own urges for cultural criticism. It is struggling to forge a more politicized humanism. The older humanist paradigms seem manifestly naive and irrelevant, so much so that a vexed question looms for the whole literary culture: how can a humanism, however politicized, fail to seem so? The stance Rushdie has chosen, drawing on and echoing diverse literary and critical strands—surrealist manifestoes, Bakhtin, to name just two—is one effort to answer this question. The irreverent, blaspheming polemical potential provided by the familiarizing speech of popular culture, the "carnival" that "marks the suspension of all hierarchical ranks, privileges, norms and prohibitions," that "opposes all that is ready-made and completed, all pretence at immutability"[17]—these are the explicit adoptions of an answer that attempts, on the one hand, to move out of existing apolitical formalisms and relativisms, and on the other, to finesse the outdated, pious, legitimizing modes of traditional humanisms. The answer may not, in the end, satisfy, and undoubtedly there are other possible answers. On that I take no particular stand, at any rate not here. But it is *an* answer, and Rushdie's critics should acknowledge that novels that struggle to provide such answers are struggling with one of the most urgent demands of their culture.

I have spent this essay defending a book against a range of criticisms from a variety of sources. The defense is of a book. If someone were to say, why if you defend this book, do you not defend the invasions of

Afghanistan and Iraq, for which similar claims might be made—that is, that they were carried out to undermine fundamentalist and other forms of tyranny—my answer is not merely that those are invasions (and not books) in which thousands of innocent people have been killed, but that I do not for a moment believe that the *motives* behind those invasions were as these claims suggest. Nor do I believe, as nobody who is not utterly uninformed and devoid of common sense could, that the *consequences* of these invasions will have been to undermine Islamic fundamentalism or the terrorism associated with it. If anything, the opposite is true. Rushdie has sometimes written and spoken with sympathy about these actions of the U.S. government,[18] and the sympathy is in some sense, I suppose, intended to be continuous with his efforts in *The Satanic Verses,* to oppose Islamic fundamentalism. Nothing whatever in this essay defending that book should be seen as joining him in this sympathy. For (I wager) nothing in the arguments provided in this essay in defending that book could be continuous with any arguments that he might provide for having that sympathy.

NOTES

1. Cited in an essay on Central European art by Jonathan Jones, "The Case for Communism," *The Guardian,* May 1, 2004.

2. Salman Rushdie, *The Satanic Verses* (New York: Viking Penguin, 1989).

3. See particularly my somewhat intemperate paper "Rushdie and the Reform of Islam" in *Grand Street,* Summer 1989, written in haste and emotion on the day after the announcement of the fatwa.

4. See note 8 for the reference

5. By contrast the first argument appeals only to facts, such as that we have been wrong in the past and an induction that we may therefore be wrong at present, and derives its evaluative conclusion that we should value free speech on just these elements, and no further values. It is often called Mill's "meta-inductive" argument for free speech, thus registering the claim that anyone capable of inductive rationality (and, of course, capable of recognizing the facts) will see the force of the derivation. I have criticized this argument in the paper referred to in note 11.

6. Just a word about this use of the word *ordinary.* I have ceased using the term *moderate* Muslim partly because it sounds as if it is handing out a prize and partly because it is not clear what *immoderate* might exactly mean, given how anyone who opposes U.S. foreign policy can get counted as extremist in some circles today, leaving only the Karzais and the Musharrafs and the Chalabis as moderates. I prefer the term *ordinary* Muslims to mark out the overwhelming majority of Muslims who have no absolutist fantasies of living by sharia laws or imposing strict Islamic regimes on their people or fighting violent ideological wars against "infidels." While on terminological matters, I should also say that though I prefer the term *absolutist* to the term *fundamentalist* for describing a certain sort of Islamist

position to which I am contrasting the ordinary Muslim's Islamic commitments, I am not careful in the text above to use this preferred term throughout. I do fall into use of the term *fundamentalist* from time to time partly because it is easier to stick with the more common, if misleading, usage.

7. I repeat that Roth's remark was restricted to totalitarian states of Eastern Europe. I am simply applying it here to Islam, as it is often conceived both by the fundamentalists and by the hostile Western caricature of it. So none of these points should be taken to be a criticism of Roth, who serves here only as a dialectical foil.

8. See the exchange between them in successive issues of the *The Guardian,* November 17–22, 1997, with Christopher Hitchens joining the fray on Rushdie's side.

9. Talal Asad, *Genealogies of Reason* (Baltimore: Johns Hopkins University Press, 1993).

10. I have been putting the description "blasphemous" in scare quotes so as to mark that it is not uncontroversial as to what does or does not count as blasphemous. But no one who has read *The Satanic Verses* can seriously deny that the book contains passages that were bound to deeply offend devout Muslims. I doubt very much if the author denies it, and it would be surprising if he did not expect it.

11. I've discussed this last question at length in my "Secularism and Relativism" in a special issue on secularism of the journal *boundary 2* 31, no. 2 (2004): 173–96.

12. See "What Is a Muslim?" in *Critical Inquiry,* Summer 1992, and "Secularism and the Moral Psychology of Identity" in *Multiculturalism, Liberalism, and Democracy,* ed. A. Bagchi, R. Bhargava, and R. Sundaram (New York: Oxford University Press, 1999).

13. Michael Dummett made this criticism in a letter to the *Independent* in response to a piece I wrote there defending Rushdie on February, 14, 1990, on the anniversary of the fatwa issued against him by Imam Khomeini.

14. Despite my blanket critical remarks about a politicized Islam in the text above, I want to note that the idea (really, the ideas) of a politicized Islam has to be carefully analyzed and I do not have the space to do it here. As my brief remark about Hamas in the text hinted, there is in some cases (though by no means all) a coinciding of absolutist Islamic political commitments with very serious and deep efforts by Islamist groups to provide for certain essential services and elements of civil society as well as provide pockets of resistance against highly brutal or corrupt or elite-dominated states.

Even so, I do entirely share Rushdie's view that Islam provides a very brittle, implausible, and indeed dangerous basis for developing and implementing the political ideals of a just and free society.

15. See his short, untitled piece in Lisa Appignanesi and Sara Maitland, eds., *The Rushdie File* (Syracuse, N.Y.: Syracuse University Press, 1990).

16. See his "Post-Modernism or the Cultural Logic of Late Capitalism," *New Left Review* 146 (1984): 53–92.

17. Quoted from Mikhail Bakhtin, *Rabelais and His World,* trans. Hélène Iswolsky (Cambridge: MIT Press, 1968), 10–11.

18. See his piece in the *Washington Post* of November 1, 2002, for example, and various other op-ed pieces in the last few years in the *Guardian* and the *New York Times.*

ASHUTOSH VARSHNEY

Lasting Injuries, Recuperative Possibilities
The Trajectory of an Insufficient National Imagination

In one of the most ingenious parts of *Shame,* a political commentary on Pakistan scripted as a novel, Salman Rushdie wrote: "Pakistan may be described as a failure of the dreaming mind. . . . Perhaps the place was just insufficiently imagined."[1]

These words were written in 1983. That was also the year Benedict Anderson published *Imagined Communities,* arguably the most influential social science book on nationalism.[2] Unknown to each other, both writers, one a novelist, the other a professor of political science at Cornell University, produced an insight that was more or less similar, the insight that imaginations are central to nation-making. Before 1983, the term *imagination* did not figure centrally in the literature on nationalism; after that, it was routinely deployed, both in the humanistic and social science arguments. Nations were conventionally viewed as outcomes of the objective forces of history, and the role of imaginations and their deployment in politics was not fully appreciated.

In this essay, I want to take the idea of imagination in nation-making and nation-building seriously and would like to ask some specific questions about Pakistan. Is Rushdie right? Was Pakistan indeed insufficiently imagined? And if so, what have been the enduring consequences of the inadequacy of imagination?

But I don't wish to confine myself to the past. I also want to peer into Pakistan's future and ask: Can Pakistan be reimagined, and if so, what form might an alternative imagination take? This question is immensely important. How Pakistan's identity is reimagined will determine—substantially, if not entirely—whether the Pakistani state will contribute to the welfare of its masses and to peace in South Asia.

The insufficiency of the founding imagination has led to enduring pathologies and self-inflicted injuries in Pakistan. Rushdie's fundamental insight is not just pithy and inventive; it is also largely correct. But there is a big question that, nonetheless, crops up. It has to do with the possibilities of Pakistan's regeneration. Rushdie has often been pessimistic about it; I am not. I only have a conjecture about Pakistan's future, not a full-blown argument, but it seems to me it is a reasonable way to start a debate. A nuclear South Asia requires serious futuristic thinking.

A "Nuclear Somalia"? A "Failed State"?

Since September 11, 2001—after years of inching closer and closer to international isolation—Pakistan has returned to the family of nations as an important international actor. Its economy, faltering badly for more than a decade, has also grown at an impressive rate over the last several years. Yet the doubt that Pakistan might turn into a "failed state" has never quite disappeared. According to an assessment presented before the 2008 Pakistan elections, despite an alliance with the United States in the war on terrorism and rising economic growth rates, the odds of Pakistan's degeneration into a failed state were high.[3] According to this study, Pakistan's vulnerability to state failure was higher than Nepal's or Sierra Leone's. One does not have to agree with the details of this assessment to appreciate that in many professional circles, grave doubts continue to exist about the capacities, including that of survival, of the Pakistani state.[4] Political developments after the 2008 elections have not fundamentally altered the assessment.

In the 1960s, Pakistan as a failed state would not have mattered all that much for international security. It is Pakistan's nuclear weapons that have given these doubts an unprecedented weight and currency. In policy circles, one often hears that if Pakistan does not substantially reform its polity, the world may have to deal with a "nuclear Somalia," a term quite routinely used after 9/11. In 2005, the discovery that Abdul Qadeer Khan, the father of Pakistan's nuclear bomb and one of the most highly placed Pakistani civilians in the nuclear establishment, had created a nuclear black market and was running a parallel nuclear policy, reignited the fear of state failure. Few security establishments in the world would allow such clandestine *nuclear* activities, brazenly violating the official policy of the state, to be run for over a decade.

Security hawks in India, unbridled "realists" for long, do not particularly mind Pakistan as a nuclear Somalia, believing that Pakistan is headed that way in any case and its nuclear installations can be preemptively "taken out" before they fall under the control of terrorist organizations. Any sensible notion of probabilities, however, would argue against such "realist" confidence. Basically, no one can predict what will happen to international or South Asian security if Pakistan does become a failed state and the existing security establishment loses its hold over the nuclear arsenal.

While the possibility of state failure in Pakistan has been discussed at length in policy circles, it should be noted that scholars of South Asia have, on the whole, not entertained such a claim with any degree of seriousness. Few scholars would deny that the Pakistani state continues to suffer from a fundamental political incoherence. But to talk about a low-level equilibrium or a deep-seated political incoherence of the state is one thing. To jump from that to a comprehensive state failure is quite another.

The underlying aspects of a low-level equilibrium in Pakistan's polity are well known. Even after over six decades of independence, the basic structure of political institutions, which in a normal state would, among other things, lay out the respective spheres of civilian and military jurisdiction, remains unsettled in Pakistan. And none of the multiple constitutions of independent Pakistan has endured as a basic architecture for power arrangements. India has gone through a great deal of political turbulence, but the survival of India's 1950 constitution and the spheres of civilian and military jurisdiction in the polity have rarely been in grave doubt. The Emergency (1975–77) was the only time in Indian politics when the constitution was seriously abrogated. But even then the idea of soldiers as politicians did not raise its head, and the electoral rejection of the Emergency in March 1977 was so decisive that no political leader can easily think of suspending democracy and the constitution any more. The idea that the constitution could be undermined on any grounds has simply moved out of the institutionalized common sense of Indian politics. The Supreme Court of India, the ultimate guarantor of the constitution, has, if anything, acquired a great deal of power and legitimacy in public eyes.[5]

This comparison does speak about the ill health of political and state institutions of Pakistan, but it does not suggest that the odds of state failure are high. Central to the notion of state failure is the idea that the state is unable to provide and protect public order, and in extreme cases, its writ barely runs beyond the capital city, and warlords or tribal heads control their respective territories.[6] The latter phenomenon has often been noted in sub-Saharan Africa and also in Afghanistan, Pakistan's neighbor. Over and above the illegitimacy of civilian politicians, typically associated with state failure are factors such as unbridgeable rifts in, and collapse of, the armed forces, or the military losing mass legitimacy.

Recent surveys in Pakistan show that while the soldiers may not be favored by Pakistanis *as political rulers,* they continue to be trusted by a vast majority of people as the nation's armed forces.[7] So long as the armed forces remain reasonably united and do not lose their legitimacy as a professional organization in the eyes of the populace, the conditions of state failure are unlikely to mature in Pakistan. The implication of this argument is not that soldiers should continue to run politics; far from it. When soldiers run politics, the health of political institutions is almost inevitably undermined. The military creates an agonizing dilemma for Pakistani citizens: its frequent interference in politics contributes to a low-level equilibrium in the polity, generating anxiety about the future of Pakistan, but the fact that Pakistan's armed forces continue to enjoy legitimacy as a professional force prevents the worst-case scenario—a state implosion—from taking place. Despite the mass turbulence under Musharraf, surveys continue to show that the military in Pakistan has substantial legitimacy as an institution. The doubts that emerge now and then are essentially about its political role.[8]

Though formal military rule in Pakistan began in 1958, it is in the 1960s that military interference took deep institutional roots and a priority of soldiers over civilian politicians was first established. Compared to the 1960s, the rise of Islamism *within the state and the army* is now unmistakable, and the state has developed considerable incapacity to monitor antistate activities of state officials as well as citizen groups so long as they are couched in Islamic language. To the extent that this has created conflicting blocks and interests within the state and reduced the capacity of government to police borders, the Pakistani state today is indeed more vulnerable to failure than before, but greater vulnerability must be distinguished from inexorability. The existing state of affairs does not have to continue for ever. Change is possible.

Whatever one might say about the future of Pakistan, an important question about the past remains. Why did things come to such a pass? As in so many other cases, two kinds of reasons can be provided: the proximate, and the underlying. The proximate reasons have to do with the political events of the 1980s and 1990s, which I discuss in what follows; the underlying reasons concern the identity of Pakistan and the imagination that led to its birth, which I will discuss later.

The 1980s and 1990s

In the 1980s, under General Zia ul-Haq, the head of the armed forces as well as the government, Islam became a *driving force* of statecraft, not simply a *background factor* that the state had to consider in its functioning.[9] And in the 1990s, a crippling contradiction emerged between the security impulses of the state and the welfare of the masses. As Pakistan invested in security to keep up with India in military terms, it declined economically, socially, and politically. A descent into military rule is only too well known, but the economic and social story is equally disastrous.

Between 1988 and 1999, Pakistan's rate of economic growth averaged a little over half of India's.[10] In terms of growth in GNP per capita, the difference was even more pronounced. Given Pakistan's considerably higher population growth rate, India's GNP per capita growth rate was four times higher each year.[11] In the same period, the percentage of population below the line of poverty roughly doubled in Pakistan.[12] In India, the absolute magnitude of poverty remained a cause of concern, but the percentage of those below the poverty line declined.

The comparison on education, too, brings no favor to Pakistan. Following Amartya Sen, a lot of Indians are justifiably critical of their country's educational performance. But if the comparison is with Pakistan, Indian performance begins to look quite good. In 2003, Pakistan's rate of adult literacy was roughly 49 percent, India's 61 percent.[13] In 2003, only 35 percent of Pakistan's adult women were literate; in India, the proportion was 48 percent. Thus, India's literacy profile also shows a considerable gender imbalance, but the gender gap in Pakistan is virtually unparalleled. In Asia, only Nepal and Bangladesh have lower female literacy rates, and Bangladesh seems to be quickly catching up with Pakistan.

Finally, and most critically of all, in the 1990s, development spending in Pakistan's budget fell dramatically, but defense spending increased.[14] As Noman noted in 2001: "Pakistan is part of an arms race that it can ill afford. Others engaged in it have rising incomes and lowering poverty."[15] A preoccupation with defense and security became one of the principal reasons for Pakistan's economic and social failures. In a declining economic scenario, the more it spent on defense, the less it had for developmental expenditures. The poor masses paid a high price for Pakistan's search for military parity with India.

By 2000–2001, for all practical purposes, the Pakistani state had become a national security state, caring about and paying attention to little else. It faced roughly the same dilemma that the Soviet Union did in the 1980s: namely, could an economically declining Pakistan continue to play the game of military parity with an economically resurgent India, just as the Soviets did with the United States? Luckily, the economic turnaround appears to have begun, and an Indo-Pak peace process, with all its hiccups, has also been under way. Assuming that these two newer trends continue, the question—will Pakistan implode the way the Soviet Union did?—will no longer be relevant. The possibility of state implosion was premised upon an unending hostility with India and a continued economic stagnation. Of course, if Pakistan's economic fortunes falter again, the older questions will come back with considerable force and intensity.

If the conditions of the 1980s and 1990s leading to Pakistan's decline are transparently clear and have been written about at length,[16] what about the underlying reasons? Is there a prism through which we can view the political evolution of Pakistan right since its birth as a nation? Is there a set of central ideas that facilitates linking the various problems, which may otherwise appear to be dauntingly formless?

Since its birth in 1947, Islam and anti-Indianism have been the two master narratives of Pakistan's polity. Islam itself has taken two forms: as a cultural idea, and as a religious one. But in both forms, Islam's power to unite Pakistan's disparate communities has fallen short. In the end, anti-Indianism, albeit suffused with a touch of ambivalence, has turned out to be a stronger uniting force.

India's cultural life and heroes have always been a source of attraction in Pakistan, just as many of Pakistani cultural icons have traveled remarkably well in India. Many personal friendships across the border have also blossomed. But these notes of social or personal warmth have never overpowered the reasons of the state. Islam could have been a binding and positive force for Pakistan, if only it had greater plausibility. Anti-Indianism, as a consequence, becomes a default option for national cohesion. For reasons discussed later, the Indian state has had to rely less on an anti-Pakistan impulse.

Islam: Culture or Religion?

It is sometimes suggested that yet another discussion of Jinnah's two-nation theory simply fatigues Pakistanis and reduces the possibility of a fruitful discussion about how to improve relations between Indian and Pakistan. The underlying logic of this assertion is that an attack on the founding principles of a state is no way to build warmth and civility.

Whatever the validity of this position from a *policy* perspective, it is a nonstarter from an *analytic* perspective. It is not clear how to begin an analysis of Pakistan's political evolution without a discussion of the two-nation theory. Many of Pakistan's past and ongoing troubles are intimately tied up with Jinnah's argument about why two nations—India and Pakistan—were needed in the first place.

In its original formulation, South Asian Islam—as a cultural, not a religious, idea—was to be the core of Pakistan's national identity. Pakistan was born as a Muslim state, not as an Islamic one. With the exception of one clerical school (the Barelvis), all schools of Islamic theology in British India were opposed to the idea of Pakistan. Theologically, Islam provided the foundation for an *umma,* an international community, not a national one. Moreover, the clerics found the idea of an utterly westernized leader, Mohammed Ali Jinnah, leading the Muslims of South Asia quite preposterous.

Jinnah, indeed, had no patience for an Islamic state, or for the clerics. In the famous Lahore Resolution of 1940, which became the intellectual bedrock of Pakistan, his argument was cultural:

> Islam and Hinduism . . . are not religions in the strict sense of the word, but are in fact different and distinct social orders.
> . . . [T]hey belong to two different civilizations which are based mainly on conflicting ideas and conceptions. . . . They have different epics, (and) their heroes are different. . . . Very often, the hero of one is the foe of the other and likewise their victories and defeats overlap.[17]

The Muslims, according to this doctrine, could not expect fairness and justice in an independent India, where the Hindus, their adversaries, would constitute a majority. Muslims had to build a political roof over their cultural heads, and take full control of their destinies. They were not simply a religious, but a distinct cultural and national, community.

The two-nation theory, of course, did not go uncontested. Reading Indian history differently, Maulana Azad, another Muslim stalwart of the first half of the twentieth century, a scholar of religious texts, and a leader of the Congress Party, vigorously argued that being a Muslim did not require denial of Indian heritage.

> I am a Muslim and proud of that fact. Islam's splendid traditions of thirteen hundred years are my inheritance. . . . In addition, I am proud of being an Indian. I am part of the indivisible unity that is Indian nationality. . . .
>
> It was India's historic destiny that many human races and cultures and religious faiths should flow to her, and that many a caravan should find rest here. . . . One of the last of these caravans was that of the followers of Islam. . . .
>
> . . . Eleven centuries have passed by since then. Islam has now as great a claim on the soil of India as Hinduism. If Hinduism has been the religion of the people here for several

thousand years, Islam has also been their religion for a thousand years. . . .

Eleven hundred years of common history have enriched India with our common achievement. Our languages, our poetry, our literature, our culture, our art, our dress, our manners and customs, the innumerable happenings of our daily life, everything bears the stamp of our joint endeavour. There is indeed no aspect of our life, which has escaped this stamp.[18]

That Jinnah's argument did not fully succeed has, in retrospect, become Pakistan's biggest structural problem as a nation. Jinnah simply could not win over the entire Muslim community of British India. It is arguable, though not entirely provable—counterfactuals rarely are—that if the two-nation theory had succeeded, Pakistan would have overcome its anti-Indianism over time. The success of the two-nation theory could well have become a source of psychological security. Nations not troubled about their identity are often less externally involved and more internally calm. Of course, whether the two-nation theory, given the serious internal cleavages of South Asian Muslims, would at all have succeeded is another matter. In that sense, Rushdie's point about insufficient imagination is right. Islam was used by Jinnah, among other things, to cover the internal diversities of Indian Muslims, but the divisions were too deep to remain hidden and dormant for long.[19] Something other than Islam was needed for nation-building.

The two-nation theory has faced formidable challenges right since its birth. Facts on the ground have rarely given it a long and enduring moment of empirical comfort. To begin with, unlike India's freedom movement, in which Gandhi, Nehru, and the Congress Party had untiringly mobilized the masses for almost three decades, the political movement for Pakistan lasted a mere seven years before the movement—for a whole variety of reasons—acquired a state of its own in 1947. Few nations in the world have had such short gestation periods. Muslim masses were not mobilized on behalf of the theory; only the tiny Muslim middle classes of British India were. The Muslim League, leading the Pakistan movement, did handsomely win Muslim endorsement in the last election (1946) of British India, but the franchise at that time was strictly confined to the educated and the propertied. No reasonable statistical imputations would put the number of Muslim voters at significantly more than 10–12 percent of the total Muslim population in 1946. Essentially, the nation of Pakistan came into being even before its mass base was established.

The followers of the two-nation theory sometimes use the horrific violence during India's partition as evidence that Hindus and Muslims could not live with each other and the two-nation theory had mass legitimacy, not simply the approval of educated and propertied Muslims. Why otherwise would so many Hindus and Muslims brutally kill each other? This argument is a *non sequitur*. It derives causes from consequences. The violence only proved that once partition was accepted, unspeakable havoc was unleashed on the masses, even though they had little to do with its creation. Postpartition violence cannot demonstrate that partition was a voluntary choice of the Muslim masses on an ideational, or ideological, basis.

As India and Pakistan commenced their independent journeys, the two-nation theory received further blows. The unwillingness of the highly popular Muslim leaders of a Muslim-majority Kashmir, stalwarts such as Sheikh Abdullah, to join Pakistan was the first crippling disappointment;[20] and the reasonable success of India as a democracy under Nehru in the 1950s, despite the odds against such a success raised by the violent horrors of partition, increasingly suggested the viability of a multireligious India. It was, moreover, an India that seemed quite comfortable with a constitutional and democratic framework of politics. In contrast, Pakistan found it impossible even to devise a constitution until 1956, and in the first of several iterations of the same phenomenon, the 1956 constitution was abrogated in 1958. Finally, the first national multiparty elections in Pakistan could not be held until the late 1960s. India had had four national elections by then.

In 1972, the birth of a Muslim-majority Bangladesh as a nation, breaking away from Pakistan, wrote the epitaph of the two-nation theory. The presumed cohesion of the Muslims of British India was eaten away by their interminable inner conflicts and diversities. There was nothing surprising about this sad denouement. *South Asian Islam is fundamentally multicultural.* To emphasize the religious commonality and to suppress the cultural diversity under a religious banner was the kind of flattening of multiple identities that Bengali Muslims would not easily accept. They were not simply Muslim, but also proudly Bengali. Both parts of the identity were important and had to coexist.

The point, of course, is not confined to Bangladesh or Muslims. If Hindu nationalists try to turn India into a Hindu nation, a homeland only of the Hindus, they will also come to grief. Cultural identity envisioned as a religious identity is too narrow a view of culture for most people in South Asia, and too restrictive a view of identity. As Sen has argued, oversimplified singularities, if imposed by the elite from above, can be a source of ghastly violence in a necessarily complex and multi-layered world of identities.[21]

The conduct of most Indian Muslims after 1947 has also been a living refutation of the theory. By fighting for India in the armed forces against Pakistan, and vigorously participating in the public sphere—sports, films, music, art, and business (especially in western and southern India)—India's Muslims have time and time again demonstrated that they do not have an adversarial relationship with the Indian nation. To be sure, the treatment of the Muslim minority in India is not entirely satisfactory; Muslims are more often than not the target of violence in riots, they are also among the most impoverished; and much can be done to improve matters.[22] But the constitution, law, and politics continue to pay attention to Muslim concerns, and despite the attempts of Hindu nationalists to rewrite Indian history, the dominant interpretation of Indian history and culture continues to show that pluralism and syncretism marked India's social and religious identities.[23] Hindu-Muslim riots, often presented in Pakistan as indicative of an irreparable rift between the two communities and a sign of the Hindu oppression of Muslims, are highly localized in India, not a feature of Hindu-Muslim relations all over the country.[24]

In the 1980s, the two-nation theory was given a new twist in Pakistan. President Zia, the then ruler of Pakistan, gave up Jinnah's idea of *Islam as culture*. Instead, *Islam as religion* became an explicit basis of state policy and conduct. Right through the first two decades of Pakistan's existence, the relationship of Islamic religiosity and the state was shot through with profound ambivalence. A religious man himself, Zia decided to end that.

The most exhaustive account yet of Pakistan state's functioning in the 1980s (as also later in the 1990s) suggests the following developments: a rising Islamic presence in the army, an institution that used to be historically secular; a striking inability of the armed forces to concede power to the civilians, except under great mass political pressure or external duress, especially from the United States; and the emergence of multiple centers of power, some committed to Islamism, others to secular anti-Indianism, and still others seeking to combine the two.[25] The state under President Zia systematically promoted Islamism within the state, the legal structures, the armed forces, the intelligence apparatus, and the nation's education system.[26]

Even this religious turn was unable to repair deep social divisions. First, riding on the argument that those who led the movement for Pakistan, Muslims from India during the 1940s, were being treated shabbily in the nation they had created, a powerful Muhajir movement emerged in Sindh. The movement took a violent turn, reducing Karachi, the nation's commercial capital, into a city virtually perpetually on the boil, and leading to a huge loss of lives. Second, the Shia-Sunni divide became deeper and violent. The militia of both religious sects got locked into a cycle of reprisal and counterreprisals, a cycle from which they have yet to emerge fully.[27] Finally, blessed by the United States, which was fighting Soviet occupation of Afghanistan, and promoted by the Pakistani state under the religiously driven policies of General Zia, large organizations of armed religious militants were born, acquiring muscle, protection, and ambition. First they sought to throw out the unbelieving Communists from Afghanistan, and then they turned their guns toward Kashmir, where India's shortsighted policies had led to an internal rebellion. What has come to be called religious terrorism was born in such circumstances in Pakistan, and its impact is still being felt. As far as the official policy pronouncements go, the Pakistani state has fought these groups, but it is also clear that such groups had the support of many at the upper echelons of the Pakistani state. Instead of developing a coherent purpose, the state became Janus-faced.[28] It is too early to say that the government formed after the 2008 elections has fundamentally transformed the two-sided character of the state's functioning.

In short, both the cultural and religious interpretations of Islam have been insufficient for national unity. Anti-Indianism has ipso facto become a much larger source for national cohesion. Compared to Islam, a struggle with India over Kashmir simply brings out greater national purpose, uniting both those who are driven by a religious impulse and those not religiously inclined.

Anti-Indianism

Pakistani scholars and intellectuals have often commented that it was Jinnah's belief that once Pakistan came into existence, peace between India and Pakistan would be the natural state of affairs. That this did not happen is sometimes ascribed to India's implacable hostility to Pakistan as a separate and independent state, an attitude that, according to these scholars, goes back to India's first prime minister, Jawaharlal Nehru. By this logic, Pakistan's anti-Indianism is a reactive phenomenon, nothing more.

For most Indians, this argument has always lacked credibility. If Nehru could not be trusted to deliver, who could be? That Nehru was fundamentally opposed to the two-nation theory did not mean he was also hostile to the nation born out of a Congress-Muslim League agreement to which he was party. Nor was hostility toward Pakistan in Nehru's interest. Containing communalism in India was one of the abiding features of Nehru's political project. Peace with Pakistan aided that project; hostility did not. That was certainly true in the circumstances of the 1950s and early 1960s.

In the end, the issue is not whether Nehru was trustworthy, or any of the other Indian leaders were, or what for that matter their attitudes were. *A certain level of anti-Indianism is written into the psychological and historical foundations of Pakistan.* It is not a matter of will or volition. There was always an India, culturally, if not politically, and there was never a Pakistan before 1947. At best, we can stretch the idea of Pakistan—culturally and politically—back to the thoughts of the great poet Iqbal in the late 1920s and early 1930s.[29]

The relative historical infancy of the idea of Pakistan has serious implications: Pakistan draws one its primary rationales from the argument that it is *not India*. India's freedom movement did not break away from Pakistan; the Pakistan movement sought separation from India, arguing an independent India would be unfair and unjust to Muslims and be inevitably inclined toward Hindu majoritarianism, despite the protestations of India's leading political figures to the contrary. Given this background, Pakistan's history books, its statecraft, and its attempts at building a national consciousness had to reflect the assumption that went into the birth of Pakistan. Stated differently, take away anti-Indianism, and Pakistan as a nation loses a key component of its national identity, if not the only component, and a principal pillar of its national cohesion, if not the only pillar. Maintaining hostility toward India was a fairly natural mode of nation-building.

Pakistani intellectuals often find the line between anti-Indianism and nation-building troubing or unacceptable. We should however note that this process is not altogether unique. Historical scholarship shows that several nations in Europe were also built this way. In her pathbreaking work, Colley has argued that without a Catholic France as enemy, it would have been enormously difficult to bring the Scots, Welsh, and English together into a British nation.[30]

The Scottish-English relationship was adversarial right until the middle of the eighteenth century. The Scots and the English, Colley argues, "came to define themselves as a single people not because of any political or cultural consensus at home, but rather in reaction to the Other beyond their shores."[31] Further, "Time and time again, war with France brought Britons, whether they hailed from Wales or Scotland or England, into a confrontation with an obviously hostile Other and encouraged them to define themselves against it. They defined themselves as Protestants struggling for survival against the world's foremost Catholic power."[32]

Pakistan's nation-building problems, thus, have historical parallels. The key difference, of course, is that Britain was not nuclear in the eighteenth century, nor was France. India and Pakistan simply cannot wait as long as Britain and France did to manage their enmity, while fighting wars in the interim.

Except when it is under a Hindu nationalist domination, India does not need an antithetical attitude toward Pakistan to justify its nationhood. In its founding ideology, it was envisioned as a multireligious, multicultural nation. Living a multireligious, multicultural ideal has not been easy, as it rarely is, and there are still battles to be fought, especially against the Hindu nationalist conception of India. But by all comparative standards, India's multiculturalism is at the very least a half-success.[33]

A Different Future?

Is the integral link between anti-Indianism and Pakistan's national identity a reason for despair? Surprising as it may seem, the link lends itself to some ideas for peace.[34]

To begin with, we need an alternative imagination. The new imagination should not be diametrically opposed to the history of Pakistan, or it will be stillborn. Lohia socialists in India have always talked of an India-Pakistan *mahasangh,* a sort of loose binational confederation. Many citizen groups also think that if the state could somehow be plucked out of the way, uninterrupted peace and friendship will descend. These romantic notions have no possibility of life in the real world. The state will not wither away; groups that substantially derive their power and status from anti-Indianism, the military and the religious organizations, will not disappear.

How, then, should we rethink? A paradox that has remained mostly unexplored, or has at best been at the periphery of intellectual debates, is in need of resurrection. *The relative improbability of friendship between the two states should be the foundation of peace initiatives, not the expectation of profound warmth or intimacy.* The potency of anti-Indianism in the very existence of Pakistani state must be seen as a constant, not as a variable. Individuals in India and Pakistan can be friends, but the two states cannot develop bracing warmth, only working civility, in the foreseeable future. Peace between India and Pakistan should not be conceptualized as the dawn of friendship; it should simply be seen as the end of hostilities. If anti-Indianism, more than Islam, brings Pakistan's many and fractious political and ethnic groups together, it is pointless to try to force artificial cordiality between the two nations. It will not last. We have to recognize that Indo-Pak cordiality threatens the basic foundations of two hugely powerful groups in Pakistan, the armed forces and the religious organizations.

For peace to move more resolutely forward, the power of these groups first has to be curbed. Short of defeats in war, unthinkable in a nuclear South Asia, only democracy can restrain the power of these groups in Pakistan. Civilian politicians in the past may have brought disrepute to themselves, but military rule is no solution to Pakistan's fundamental problems. More than half of Pakistan's independent life has been spent under military rule, and Pakistan's search for prosperity, international status, and political coherence is still nowhere close to fruition. In 2008, another democratic opening has emerged. Religious political parties have been defeated, and the military is on the defensive. Democracy in Pakistan will continue to disempower these two groups. The critical issue is whether democracy will last.

Second, the alternative idea for the rebuilding of Pakistan should not depart fundamentally from its founding imagination, however insufficient the original version was. The trick is to reinvent a different version of the same idea. Pakistan needs to reimagine, and institutionalize, India-Pakistan rivalry as a thoroughgoing *competition,* not as a do-or-die *conflict.* A distinction needs to be drawn between two terms: adversaries and enemies. Adversaries can be respected, even admired; enemies are killed. India and Pakistan must cease to be enemies; they need to become adversaries competing vigorously to become better than the other.

Is this simply a logical and conceptual distinction, or are there some real-world models that come to mind? After the peace summit of 1999 between India's prime minister Vajpayee and Pakistan's prime minister Nawaz Sharif, a summit that laid the foundation of the current peace process, Haqqani writes, "Sharif voiced the hope, first expressed by Pakistan's founder Muhammad Ali Jinnah days before partition, that 'Pakistan and India will be able to live as the United States and Canada.'"[35]

Haqqani did not elaborate any further on this insight, but the idea of U.S.-Canadian relations as a model for India and Pakistan is both intriguing and one potentially filled with imaginative as well as pragmatic possibilities. And the fact that Jinnah apparently thought of it gives it a usable authenticity for Pakistan's future restructuration.

As we know, a certain level of anti-Americanism is part of Canada's national psyche: Canada, says a Canadian writer, "seeks to unify its chronically fractured sense of nationhood in opposition to the United States."[36] Yet the resentments have always coexisted with admiration for the United States. An oft-cited survey showed that 70 percent of Canadians like the United States and only 15 percent completely dislike the United States and its people.[37]

Moreover, Canadians never cease to take pride in what makes them different from the United States: a national health insurance system, reflecting a society that is more compassionate than the United States, where as of April 2008, 40–45 million citizens were without health insurance; a model of nation-building consciously defined as a mosaic, not as a melting pot, as in the United States; a commitment to multilateralism in foreign policy; laws showing greater environmental consciousness than in the United States; greater secularism as opposed to the well-known religiosity of the United States; a pacific tradition as against the muscular and martial fervor often evident in the U.S. public discourse and foreign policy. Every now and then, an economic discovery that beats competition in the United States, such as the invention of the BlackBerry, can also be part of that pride, but Canadians know that their economy has not been as inventive as that of the United States. That, however, has not undermined their national image, for there are so many other ways of seeking difference and taking pride in achievements.

Finally, Canada has the kind of anti-Americanism that has not come in the way of either Canadian prosperity or economic relations with the United States. "A truck crosses the US-Canadian border every 2.5 seconds. Approximately, $1.3 billion in two-way trade crosses the border every day—or $500 billion a year. More than 200 million two-way border crossings occur yearly, making the shared border the busiest international boundary in the world."[38]

Peace in South Asia requires a threefold strategy: (a) commitment of both India and Pakistan to the various modes of crisis management, without expecting an absence of crises; (b) institutionalization of democracy in Pakistan; (c) the rechanneling of the anti-Indian aspects of Pakistan's identity in a positive direction. The first part of the strategy, the main thrust of international diplomatic action in recent years, is about firefighting; the second and third parts, not yet the main thrust, are about a long-run strategy for reducing the probability that fires will break out.

The U.S.-Canadian relationship offers a model for the long-term vision. Military victories are not the only way for a nation to raise its international profile and gain a sense of security. A competitive fervor in various spheres of life—cultural, economic, intellectual, social—is a win-win game, from which both nations can benefit. In contrast, military competition normally leads to a zero-sum game. The victory of one is the defeat of the other. Pakistan wants a Muslim-majority Kashmir because that way it can avenge the loss of Bangladesh and redeem pride. A victory in Kashmir would also, partially if not fully, restore the badly wounded two-nation theory.

We know, however, that India will not abandon Kashmir, for the loss of Kashmir, its only Muslim-majority state, will seriously undermine India's multireligious foundations and make India's Muslims highly vulnerable to a Hindu right-wing hysteria. The latter is a source of embarrassment to Indian liberals, but politics on such highly charged matters is rarely, if ever, driven by liberalism or by the normative excellence of ideas. Faced with hysteria on nation-making or nation-breaking, liberals are often helpless.

Be that as it may, with nuclear weapons on both sides, the battle over Kashmir is no longer "winnable." It is almost certain to be a stalemate, while the costs, economic and human, of a low-intensity conflict can only mount. This does not mean that for the sake of nuclear realism, the status quo in Kashmir should be maintained. At a minimum, a political regime more hospitable to human rights in Jammu and Kashmir and greater movement of Kashmiris across the line of control are necessary. But that is very different from changing existing lines of sovereignty.

The withering experience of the latest round of military rule in Pakistan is causing much rethinking in policy and intellectual circles. The message that needs to be emphasized is that Pakistan should keep trying to defeat India in other spheres of life, not on the military battlefield. This requires not only a continued economic recovery and expansion, but also, among other things, building a credible mainstream school system—to neutralize the attraction of madrasas and to nurture twenty-first-century skills in Pakistani youth. For long-term national renewal, Pakistan's education system, badly neglected thus far, requires careful attention. India also has its educational problems, but they are not as serious.

A security obsession with India has thrown Pakistan into such a profound political and economic abyss that its leadership needs to think afresh. Despite security concerns, Indian economy has been booming for quite some time and its democracy also continues to function, but in Pakistan a preoccupation with security has seriously hurt the economic development process and has, even more critically, led to awfully weakend political institutions, raising fears of state failure. Pakistan's Indian obsession has become utterly self-destructive.

For peace in the subcontinent, Pakistan needs to reinvent the nature of its anti-Indianness, not abandon its anti-Indianness per se. This idea for peace recognizes Pakistan's structural need for an adversary for national cohesion in the foreseeable future, but it also seeks to link that need to mass welfare. Pakistani masses have paid an awful price for the obsession of their state with security. They deserve better.

NOTES

This chapter was put through an online seminar by Lloyd Rudolph. The discussion was vigorous. I am especially grateful to Anis Dani, Husain Haqqani, Vali Nasr, Lloyd Rudolph, and Maya Tudor for their comments.

1. *Shame* (New York: Picador, 1983), 92. For another discussion of the theme of insufficient imagination, see Philip Oldenburg, "A Place Insufficiently Imagined? Language, Belief, and the Pakistan Crisis of 1971," *Journal of Asian Studies* 44, no. 4 (1985): 711–33.

2. Benedict Anderson, *Imagined Communities: Reflections on the Origin and Spread of Nationalism* (London: Verso, 1983).

3. "The Failed State Index," *Foreign Policy,* May–June 2006. Also see the collection of articles under the heading "State Failure" in *National Interest,* March–April 2008.

4. For expressions of deep anxiety, see Owen Bennet Jones, *Pakistan: Eye of the Storm* (New Haven: Yale University Press, 2002); and Hassan Abbas, *Pakistan's Drift into Extremism* (Armonk, NY: M. E. Sharpe, 2005).

5. Peter R. deSouza, "Political Trust, Institutions, and Democracy in India, Pakistan and Sri Lanka," paper prepared for the World Bank conference "Rethinking Social Policy in the Developing and Transition Economies," Arusha, Tanzania, December 12–15, 2005; Lloyd Rudolph and Susanne Rudolph, "Redoing the Constitutional Design: From an Interventionist to a Regulatory State," in *The Success of India's Democracy,* ed. Atul Kohli (New York: Cambridge University Press, 2001).

6. Sometimes, the incapacity of the state to provide basic education and health to its citizens is also defined as an essential component of state failure. If we define state failure so broadly, India is also a failed state. India's educational and health record, though not as bad as Pakistan's, is rather poor. Such broad definitions typically do not go to the core of the problem.

7. DeSouza, "Political Institutions."

8. For a succinct overview of the role of the army in Pakistan's politics, see Stephen Cohen, *The Idea of Pakistan* (Washington, D.C.: Brookings Institution, 2004), chap. 3.

9. For a detailed and insightful account, see Husain Haqqani, *Pakistan: Between Mosque and Military* (Washington, D.C.: Carnegie Endowment for International Peace, 2005), chap. 4.

10. Growth was 3.6 percent per year for Pakistan as compared to 6.9 percent for India in the same period. Unless otherwise indicated, the statistics for the 1990s come from United Nations Devlopment Programme's *Human Development Report*

2000 and the World Bank's *World Development Report 2000/2001,* both published by Oxford University Press. It is generally believed that compared to India, Pakistan's economy did much better roughly till the mid-1980s. It was also sometimes postulated that Pakistan had the potential to become an "economic tiger." See Omar Noman, *Economic and Social Progress in South Asia: Why Pakistan Did Not Become a Tiger* (New York: Oxford University Press, 1998).

11. For Pakistan the per capita income growth was 1.2 percent per year, for India 4.5 percent. Moreover, despite being roughly at the same per capita income level as India in the 1980s and 1990s, Pakistan saved and invested very little. Pakistan had a savings rate of 12.7 percent of GDP and an investment rate of 17.1 percent in 1998; for India, the figures were 20.9 percent and 23.6 percent respectively

12. The proportion below the poverty line in Pakistan *rose* from 17.3 percent in 1987 to nearly 32.6 percent in 1998.

13. These figures are from *Human Development Report 2005.*

14. In 1991, in *nominal* terms, development spending was 9.5 billion rupees and the defense spending 7.5 billion rupees. By 1999, in nominal terms again, development spending had barely risen to 9.8 billion rupees, but defense expenditures had climbed up to a whopping 14.3 billion rupees. In *real* terms, development spending fell from 28 percent of GDP in 1991 to almost its half, 15 percent in 1999. The statistics are from Omar Noman, "Economy of Conflict: The Consequences for Human Security in a Fragile Muslim Society," paper presented at the Asia Society, New York, October 16, 2001.

15. Noman, "Economy of Conflict."

16. The most recent account is Haqqani, *Pakistan.*

17. Jamil-ud-Din Ahmed, ed, *Some Recent Speeches and Writings of Mr. Jinnah* (Lahore: Ashraf, 1952), 1:138.

18. Maulana Azad's speech as president of the Congress Party in 1940, reproduced in *Sources of Indian Tradition,* ed. Stephen Jay, 2nd ed. (New Delhi: Penguin, 1991), 2:237–41.

19. That Islam was simply a strategic device for Jinnah is an argument forcefully made by Ayesha Jalal, *The Sole Spokesman* (Cambridge: Cambridge University Press, 1985).

20. For details, Ashutosh Varshney, "India, Pakistan and Kashmir: Antinomies of Nationalism," *Asian Survey,* November 1991.

21. Amartya Sen, *Identity and Violence: The Illusion of Destiny* (New York: W. W. Norton, 2006).

22. See Sachar Committee Report, *Social, Economic and Educational Status of the Muslim Community of India* (Delhi: Government of India, 2006).

23. As forcefully argued by Amartya Sen, *The Argumentative Indian* (New York: Farrar, Straus and Giroux, 2005).

24. Ashutosh Varshney, *Ethnic Conflict and Civic Life: Hindus and Muslims in India* (New Haven: Yale University Press, 2002).

25. Haqqani, *Pakistan.*

26. Also relevant here is the argument by made by Nasr that Malaysia and Pakistan were faced with rising Islamism from below roughly at the same time. Pakistan under Zia embraced the religious extremists, and eventually ran the nation's economy down; Malaysia under Mahathir embraced moderate Islam, and took

Malaysia toward great economic success. Nasr's claim is that Islamism and economic success can be combined. Much depends on what kind of Islam the state elects to promote. See Seyyed Vali Reza Nasr, *Islamic Leviathan: Islam and the Making of State Power* (New York: Oxford University Press, 2001).

27. For an insightful analysis of Pakistan's Shia-Sunni violence, see Seyyed Vali Reza Nasr, "International Politics, Domestic Imperatives, and Identity Mobilization: Sectarianism in Pakistan, 1979–1998," *Comparative Politics* 32, no. 2 (January 2000): 171–90.

28. See Haqqani, *Pakistan,* chap. 7.

29. Some take it all the way back to Sir Syed Ahmed Khan and his creation of the Aligarh College. That is conceptually incorrect. Aligarh may have been the institutional centerpiece of the Pakistan movement, but Sir Syed was essentially a prenational thinker. His attempt was to ensure that after the British suppression of the 1857 mutiny, which symbolized the end of Mughal rule in Delhi, the Muslim community, by which he nearly always meant *Muslim aristocrats,* did not decline any further. Modern education, he argued, was the tool for arresting aristocratic decline. There was no room for *poor Muslims* in his conceptualization of Muslim progress. The quest for Pakistan as a separate nation, thus, cannot be linked to Sir Syed, even if the institution he created ended up playing such an important role in the making of Pakistan. Historically, as Benedict Anderson has powerfully reminded us, nationalism was fundamentally opposed to the preexisting dynastic forms of rule and privilege. It sought a more horizontal notion of political community, which aristocrats typically fought against.

30. Linda Colley, *Britons: Forging the Nation, 1707–1837* (New Haven, Yale University Press, 1992). In addition to France as an enemy, Colley adds two more factors to British nation-making: profits from trade and British empire. For the Scots especially, she argues, the colonies were extremely important: "A British imperium . . . enabled Scots to feel themselves peers of the English in a way . . . denied them in an island kingdom" (129–30).

31. Colley, *Britons,* 6.

32. Colley, *Britons,* 5.

33. For the links between multiculturalism and Indian federalism, see Amit Ahuja and Ashutosh Varshney, "Antecedent Nationhood, Subsequent Statehood: Explaining the Relative Success of Indian Federalism," in *Sustainable Peace,* ed. Philip Roeder and Donald Rothchild (Ithaca, N.Y.: Cornell University Press, 2005).

34. For some other recent discussions of the future of Pakistan, see Cohen, *The Idea of Pakistan,* chap. 8; and Haqqani, *Pakistan,* chap. 8.

35. Haqqani, *Pakistan,* 249. The last line in the Haqqani passage is quoted from a report filed by the *Washington Post*'s reporter present on the occasion: Kenneth Cooper, "India, Pakistan Kindle Hope for Peace," *Washington Post,* February 21, 1999.

36. Dan Dunsky, "Canada's Three Solitudes," *National Interest,* Winter 2005–6.

37. Dunsky, "Canada's Three Solitudes," 96.

38. Dunsky, "Canada's Three Solitudes," 94.

HUSAIN HAQQANI

Inhospitable Homeland
Salman Rushdie and Pakistan

> I think a commonplace experience of the migrant is the need
> to dispense with [the] idea of home. You simply have to do
> without it.
>
> —Salman Rushdie

Of all the countries Salman Rushdie could have called home, Pakistan
is clearly his least favorite. For their part, most Pakistanis also make it
clear that they do not like Rushdie. Islamist hardliners in Pakistan were
the first to agitate against *Satanic Verses,* and their violent protests
against the book, egged on by the country's intelligence service, pre-
ceding the unfortunately famous fatwa against Rushdie issued by Iran's
Ayatollah Khomeini. Pakistan's vernacular press often described, and
continues to describe, Rushdie as "Shaitan Rushdie," substituting for
his first name the Urdu-Arabic term for Satan.

Two of Rushdie's novels, *Midnight's Children* and *Shame,* directly
deal with Pakistan. The first uses the backdrop of the partition of India
that led to Pakistan's creation, while the second deals with the evolution of Pakistan as a deeply flawed, nuclear-armed, Islamic state.
Rushdie has commented on Pakistan in several nonfiction articles and
essays as well as in numerous interviews. Communalism is the curse of
the South Asian subcontinent in his view—"the politics of religious
hatred"[1] —and to him Pakistan is both a product of communalism as
well as an entity that has exacerbated manifestations of communal sentiment across the region.

Pakistan invites Rushdie's ridicule, and he is by no means the only
intellectual to question the rationale for Pakistan as well as what it has
become. Even in 1947, Indian and Western intellectuals were either
openly hostile or lukewarm to partition. *Time* magazine, while report-
ing on the independence of India and Pakistan, wrote that "Pakistan
was the creation of one clever man, Jinnah" and compared it unfavor-
ably to the "mass movement" leading to India's independence. The
dominant Indian narrative of independence speaks of Pakistan's creation as a tragedy.

There are several contradictions in Pakistan's history that justifiably invite criticism. Pakistan was intended to save South Asia's Muslims from becoming a permanent minority in an undivided India. It never became the homeland of all of South Asia's Muslims, however. One-third of the Indian subcontinent's Muslims remained behind as a minority in Hindu-dominated India even after partition in 1947. Within twenty-four years of its creation, Pakistan underwent a second partition and, with the birth of Bangladesh, lost more than half its population, a significant portion of its territory, and an important segment of its economy. Two-thirds of the subcontinent's Muslims now live in two separate countries, Pakistan and Bangladesh, confirming the doubts expressed before independence about the practicality of the two-nation theory.

Pakistan has been described by political analysts as being on the verge of failure on several occasions in its relatively short existence. It has been ruled by its military for most of its life as an independent nation. Although it has occasionally elected leaders to office, it has yet to witness democratic transfers of power. Each change in Pakistan's government since independence has been the result of a coup d'état or a palace coup. If Pakistan's military leaders have been authoritarian, its civilian politicians have earned the reputation of being incompetent and corrupt.

Pakistan's failings have clearly influenced Rushdie's view of the country, but his dislike for Pakistan is almost visceral. He gets the feeling of "claustrophobia, of being contained"[2] in what he sees as Pakistan's near totalitarianism. He speaks of Pakistan as a "sad, strangulated nation"[3] and is clearly concerned about "the human, civil and political rights"[4] of its citizens. But his derision for the rulers and elites of Pakistan is amplified more than his sympathy for its people.

In *Shame* Pakistan's tragic leaders, the Islamist general Zia ul-Haq and the populist Zulfikar Ali Bhutto, get characters modeled after them, and Rushdie relates the saga of Zia's execution of Bhutto in his inimitable style. But even in tragedy, Rushdie finds little sympathy for Pakistan's leaders. To Rushdie these Pakistani characters do not have "the stature you can associate with high tragedy. These are people who don't deserve tragedy."[5] In an essay following Zia ul-Haq's death, Rushdie supported the notion of stability in Pakistan under representative government, and in another piece he described Benazir Bhutto and her Pakistan Peoples Party as "Pakistan's best hope." He even declared that he would have voted for Benazir Bhutto if he had a vote in Pakistan's 1988 elections. But Rushdie could not ignore her flaws and failings and noted "the faintness, the hollowness" of the hopes pinned on her. "If Benazir is the best," he wrote, "you can guess what the rest are like."[6]

Rushdie's disdain for Pakistan extends to its culture and social life as much as it applies to Pakistan's leaders. For example, he describes Bombay—"a city built by foreigners upon reclaimed land"[7] —as his "lost city"[8] but finds Karachi, the Pakistani city with a similar geography and history "boring" mainly because of its "blinkered monoculture."[9]

Interestingly, Rushdie believes he knows Pakistan better than India, having been a regular visitor to Pakistan since the age of fourteen, primarily to see his parents, who had moved to the new country. Rushdie makes his feelings about Pakistan clear. "The more I know it the less I like it,"[10] he once told an interviewer. In *Step across the Line: Collected Non-fiction, 1992–2002,* Rushdie voiced his preference for India over Pakistan:

> As a writer, I've always thought myself lucky that, because of the accidents of my family life, I've grown up knowing something of both India and Pakistan. I have frequently found myself explaining Pakistani attitudes to Indians and vice versa, arguing against the prejudices that have grown more deeply ingrained on both sides as Pakistan has drifted further and further across the sea. I can't say my efforts have been blessed with much success, or indeed that I have been an entirely impartial arbiter. I hate the way, we, Indians and Pakistanis, have become each other's others, each seeing the other as it were through a glass, darkly, each ascribing to the other the worst motives and the sneakiest natures. I hate it, but in the last analysis, I'm on the Indian side.[11]

The history of Pakistan intersects often with Rushdie's personal history, and that intersection might explain the intensity of Rushdie's views on the subject of Pakistan. Salman Rushdie was born on June 19, 1947, four days after the British announced their plan to partition the jewel in the imperial crown—India—into the Muslim majority state of Pakistan and the Hindu majority state of India. Two months after Rushdie's birth, Pakistan emerged as an independent state on August 14, 1947, marking the culmination of decades of debate and divisions among Muslims in British India about their collective future.

After the consolidation of British rule in the nineteenth century, Muslims had found themselves deprived of the privileged status they enjoyed under Mughal rule. During the Raj, some Muslim leaders embraced territorial nationalism and did not define their collective personality through religion. These *nationalist Muslims* opposed British rule and called for full participation in the Indian nationalist movement led by the Indian National Congress of Mohandas Gandhi and Jawaharlal Nehru. Others believed that Muslims had a special identity that would be erased over time by ethnic and territorial nationalism centered primarily on the Hindu majority in India.

Coalescing in the All India Muslim League and led by Mohammed Ali Jinnah, these *Muslim nationalists* asserted that India's Muslims constituted a separate nation from non-Muslim Indians and demanded the creation of a separate country in areas with a Muslim majority. British India's Muslim-majority provinces lay in its northwest and northeast, leading to Pakistan comprising at birth two wings separated by India, until the eastern wing became the new state of Bangladesh in December 1971. Pakistan's creation represented the acceptance of the two-nation theory, which had been periodically articulated long before the formal demand for a Pakistan state in 1940 but had never been fully explained in terms of how it would be applied. Pakistan's freedom struggle had been relatively short, beginning with the demand by the All India Muslim League for a separate state in 1940 and ending with the announcement of the partition plan in June 1947. While the Muslim League claimed to speak for the majority of Indian Muslims, its strongest support and most of its national leadership came from regions where the Muslims were in a minority.[12] Even after the Muslim League won over local notables in the provinces that were to constitute Pakistan, it did not have a consensus among its leaders over the future direction of the new country. Issues such as the new nation's constitutional scheme, the status of various ethno-linguistic groups within Pakistan, and the role of religion and theologians in matters of state were still unresolved at Pakistan's birth.

The Muslim League leaders had given little thought to, and made no preparations for, how to run a new country. One possible explanation is that the demand for Pakistan was "devised for bargaining purposes to gain political leverage for Muslims."[13] Jinnah had managed to pull together various elements of Muslim leadership in India, creating communal unity through ambiguity about the final goal. He was "using the demand for Pakistan to negotiate a new constitutional arrangement in which Muslims would have an equal share of power"[14] once the British left the subcontinent. Historian Ayesha Jalal has elaborated the impact of Indian Muslim politics of the time on the demand for Pakistan as well as the nature and contradictions of that demand:

Once the principle of Muslim provinces being grouped to form a separate state was conceded, Jinnah was prepared to negotiate whether that state would seek a confederation with the non-Muslim provinces, namely Hindustan, on the basis of equality at the all India level, or whether, as a sovereign state, it would make treaty arrangements with the rest of India. . . . If they were to play their role in the making of India's constitutional future, Jinnah and the Muslim League had to prove their support in the Muslim-majority provinces. Such support could not have been won by too precise a political programme since the interests of Muslims in one part of India did not suit Muslims in others. . . . Jinnah could not afford to wreck the existing structure of Muslim politics, especially since he had nothing plausible to replace it with. This is where religion came to the rescue. . . . Yet Jinnah's resort to religion was not an ideology to which he was ever committed or even a device to use against rival communities; it was simply a way of giving a semblance of unity and solidity to his divided Muslim constituents. Jinnah needed a demand that was specifically ambiguous and imprecise to command general support, something specifically Muslim though unspecific in every other respect. The intentionally obscure cry for a "Pakistan" was contrived to meet this requirement. . . . Jinnah could not afford to state precisely what the demand for "Pakistan" was intended to accomplish. If the demand was to enjoy support from Muslims in the minority provinces it had to be couched in uncompromisingly communal terms. But the communal slant to the demand cut against the grain of politics in the Muslims provinces, particularly the Punjab and Bengal, where Muslim domination over undivided territories depended upon keeping fences mended with members of other communities.[15]

The most significant impact of Jinnah's elaborate bargaining strategy was that India's Muslims demanded Pakistan without really knowing what that demand would actually result in. Another was the effort by Jinnah's critics to point out that any division of India along communal lines would inevitably have to include a division of the two major provinces, Punjab and Bengal, along similar lines.[16] A few months before independence, Khwaja Nazimuddin, who later became Pakistan's second governor-general as well as its second prime minister, candidly told a British governor that "he did not know what Pakistan means and that nobody in the Muslim League knew."[17] But what may have been a negotiating ploy had moved millions of Indian Muslims into expecting a separate country, for the running of which the Muslim leaders had made no preparations. By May 1947, Jinnah was telling a foreign visitor, "Even if 'driven into the Sind desert,' he would insist on a sovereign state."[18]

Jinnah and his colleagues in the Muslim League had not contemplated a Pakistan that did not include all of Punjab and Bengal. If the entire scheme was designed to increase the Muslims' bargaining power in post-British India, the division of India had to be between Muslim-majority provinces and Hindu-majority provinces. "Without the non-Muslim-majority districts of these two provinces [Bengal and Punjab], the [Muslim] League could not expect to bargain for parity between 'Pakistan' and Hindustan.'"[19] In the end, the Pakistan that emerged was politically and geographically quite contrary to what most of its supporters had imagined.

The process of partitioning a subcontinent along religious lines did not prove as neat as Jinnah, the lawyer, had anticipated. The entire country was plunged into communal violence, hundreds of thousands of people from both sides were butchered, and millions had to flee their homes. The territory that constituted Pakistan was India's economic backyard and could not provide trained manpower to lead the new country's administration or military. While many Muslims migrated from India to Pakistan as a result of the violence that drove Hindus and Sikhs out of Pakistan and Muslims out of parts of India, others moved to take advantage of economic and employment opportunities in the new country. Several educated Muslim families like Rushdie's, in whose life "religion took a back seat"[20] except on occasions of holy days and special observances, were divided not so much by ideology (i.e., support for or opposition to the idea of Pakistan) but the relocation of family members who secured better jobs and higher positions in the state of Pakistan.

Although Salman Rushdie was too young to witness the horrors of partition, or even to recall the debates that preceded and followed it, the division of India had a profound impact on his life. In *Step across the Line,* Rushdie points out that, in comparison to other family histories of the time, his Indian Muslim family "was fortunate. None of us was injured or killed in the partition massacres. But all our lives were changed; even the life of a boy of eight weeks and his as-yet-unborn sisters and his extant and future cousins and all our children too. None of us are who we would have been if that line had not stepped across our land."[21]

Rushdie's parents, both affluent Muslims, had decided to stay in Bombay. Rushdie describes the religious environment in his home as open, tolerant, and not in any way stringent; he states that his parents "certainly felt more like Indians than Muslims."[22] But when Rushdie returned to India after studying for three years at the Rugby School in Britain, he discovered that his parents had made the decision to follow their relatives and to move to Pakistan. The young Salman Rushdie, arriving back in India from what had been a harrowing, but ultimately successful educational venture, was shattered by the move. Trying to explain the reason for the uprooting years later, Rushdie said, "I think there were all kinds of terrible reasons like finding husbands for my sisters. They were beginning to sense discrimination in India—there was a whole series of these half-reasons."[23] Some members of Rushdie's family, especially on the maternal side, had attained significant positions in Pakistan, and one of his uncles even became a general in the increasingly powerful Pakistani military.

Rushdie, with independence and confidence gained from his three years abroad, let his parents know his strong disapproval of the move from the only home he had ever known. Bombay was for him "the most cosmopolitan, most hybrid, most hotch-potch" of Indian cities.[24] When he was one year old, a friend of his father's presented him with a block of silver on which was engraved the map of India before the partition. Rushdie carried it with him everywhere as a symbol of his love for Bombay and India. The dazzling metropolis that Rushdie had fallen in love with as a boy would stay with him for the rest of his life as well as influence his future writings. Bombay was, in Rushdie's words, "the heart of all my work."[25]

In 1983, nineteen years after his family moved to Pakistan permanently, Rushdie commented in an interview that Bombay had radically changed from the time he knew the city as a boy. He believes that "Bombay has been more or less ruined as a city; it's now an urban nightmare whereas it used to be a courtly, open, hilly, seaside city. . . . If I were to go back to India now, I would not live in Bombay, which is something I would have never said before. It still has the feeling of being my hometown, but it is no longer a place in which I feel comfortable."[26] But Pakistan, where his parents lived, was not a place Rushdie could call home, either. As a young writer, Rushdie had his first encounter with censorship in Pakistan:

> My first encounter with censorship took place in 1968, when I was twenty-one, fresh out of Cambridge and full of the radical fervor of that famous year. I returned to Karachi, where a small magazine commissioned me to write a piece about my impressions on returning home. I remember very little about

this piece (mercifully, memory is a censor, too), except that it was not at all political . . . Any way, I submitted my piece, and a couple of weeks later was told by the magazine's editor that the Press Council, the national censors, had banned it completely. Now, it so happened that I had an uncle on the Press Council, and in a very unradical, string-pulling mood I thought I'd just go and see him and everything would be sorted out. He looked tired when I confronted him. "Publication," he said immovably, "would not be in your best interest." I never found out why.[27]

Pakistan's fall to authoritarianism, a process that was completed during Rushdie's youth and around the same time that his parents moved to Pakistan, is clearly the source of his strong views about the country he never called home.

He attributes Pakistan's authoritarianism to the feudal social norms the country adopted after independence. "If you're in a country like Pakistan, which has so often been under dictatorial or almost dictatorial control," says Rushdie, "there comes a point where you can't say that this is just bad luck. You've got to ask what it is in that society that breeds those plants. I've been there at times where there weren't dictatorships, and it still felt that the air was difficult to breathe. And it had almost primarily to do with the repression (rather than oppression) of women. If you have a society that instinctively or without much question accepts such a pattern of behavior in its social code, then the switch from that to dictatorship is relatively small. They're two aspects of the same reality."[28]

Rushdie is not the only writer and intellectual with a divided legacy or inheritance to be "on the Indian side," as he describes it. Pakistan's evolution as an intolerant, insecure state has made it inhospitable for creative and imaginative minds. Pakistan's founders came from secular backgrounds—"believers" but not "insistent or doctrinaire," as Rushdie describes his parents. But the circumstances of Pakistan's creation led them to transform Pakistan into an ideological state based on religious conservatism and fundamentalism. The greatest support for Pakistan had come from Muslims living in regions that did not become part of the new state. These Muslim minority regions, now in India, also provided a disproportionate number of the Muslim League's leadership, senior military officers, and civil servants for Pakistan's early administration. Interprovincial rivalries, ethnic and language differences, and divergent political interests of various elite groups had remained dormant while Pakistan was only a demand. Now that it was a state, these became obstacles in constitution writing and political consensus building. Territorial Pakistan had tremendous difficulty in reconciling to the domination of migrants representing the hitherto vague idea of separate Muslim nationhood.

Jinnah's successors opted to patch over domestic differences in the independent country the same way that Muslim unity had been forged during the preindependence phase. They defined Pakistani national identity through religious symbolism and carried forward the hostilities between the Indian National Congress and the All India Muslim League by building India-Pakistan rivalry. The dispute over the princely state of Jammu and Kashmir and continued criticism of the idea of Pakistan by Indian politicians and scholars helped fuel the view that "India did not accept the partition of India in good faith and that, by taking piecemeal, she could undo the division."[29] The fears of dilution of Muslim identity that had defined the demand for carving Pakistan out of India became the new nation-state's identity, reinforced over time through the educational system and constant propaganda. As time went by, the definition of Pakistan's Islamic ideology became closer to the views of Islamist fundamentalists, and the Pakistani military, especially under General Zia ul-Haq, became aligned theocrats who eventually became part of Pakistan's elite alongside the feudals and westernized generals, bureaucrats, and professionals.

The evolution of Pakistan as an Islamist ideological state, coupled with the ambiguities inherent in the demand for Pakistan, led Rushdie to conclude that Pakistan was "insufficiently imagined." In *Shame,* he outlines his critique of the country's origins and development:

So it [Pakistan] was a word born in exile which then went East, was borne-across or translated and imposed itself on history; a returning migrant, settling down on partitioned land, forming a palimpsest on the past. . . . To build Pakistan it was necessary to cover up Indian history. . . . It is possible to see the subsequent history of Pakistan as a duel between two layers of time, the obscured world forcing its way back through what-had-been-imposed. It is the true desire of every artist to impose his or her vision on the world; and Pakistan, the peeling, fragmenting palimpsest, increasingly at war with itself, may be described as a failure of the dreaming mind. . . . [P]erhaps the place was just *insufficiently imagined,* a picture full of irreconcilable elements, midriffbaring immigrant saris versus demure, indigenous Sindhi shalwar-kurtas, Urdu versus Punjabi, now versus then: a miracle that went wrong.[30]

Rushdie's objections are aimed at the idea of the Pakistani state, especially as it has been imposed by the country's civil-military elite, and he does not show any hostility against Pakistan's people. But in Pakistan, state and nation are often used as synonymous terms. The relatively short campaign for Pakistan's creation, which started in 1940 and culminated in 1947, had effectively become a religious movement even though its leaders initiated it as a formula for ensuring Muslims a greater share in postindependence political power. Pakistani national identity was weak from the beginning, and the process of nation formation was made difficult by contending visions of nationhood. But Pakistan had inherited a strong state apparatus from the British in the form of its military and civil service. The state, therefore, was in a better position to define Pakistan's future than an incompletely defined nation still in search of an identity.

Pakistan's state, armed with a state ideology, continues to be Pakistan's mainstay. In fact, government, state, and nation are often interpreted in Pakistan as one and the same thing. Criticism of the government is considered an attack on the state, and any questioning of the state is seen as undermining the foundations of Pakistani nationhood. In such an environment, Rushdie's questioning of the Pakistani state's legitimacy was bound to receive an angry response from the state and from Pakistanis who are sold on the state's definition of their identities.

Ever since Rushdie achieved international recognition as an author, supporters of the Pakistani state have been uncharitable toward him to the point of being vulgar and dismissive. Maulana Kausar Niazi, a former senator and well-known cleric-politician in Pakistan, wrote a series of articles in Urdu about Rushdie and *The Satanic Verses* even before Ayatollah Khomeini issued his fatwa against Rushdie on February 14, 1989. In these articles, Niazi argued that Rushdie was a man not at peace with himself. He ridiculed his family in his first book, *Midnight's Children;* his country in his second book, *Shame;* and his religion in his third book, *The Satanic Verses.*

Niazi was wrong on all three counts. *Midnight's Children* was not Rushdie's first book. *Grimus,* published in 1975, was. Rushdie does not consider Pakistan *his* country, nor does he identify with Islam (as practiced by most) as his religion. But Niazi did not believe in letting facts to the contrary get in the way of a good religious riot. The campaign against *Satanic Verses* in Pakistan, the result of collusion between religious-political activists and Pakistan's military intelligence service, serves as a microcosm for all that Rushdie finds wrong with Pakistan.

Satanic Verses had been published a year earlier, in 1988, and no one in the Muslim world had taken notice of it until Kausar Niazi wrote his articles about it in the Pakistani press. Niazi said that a copy of the book, with offensive passages duly highlighted, had been sent to him by a senior official in the Pakistan Inter-Services Intelligence (ISI), the country's secret police and intelligence service.[31] Niazi had been minister for religious Affairs in Zulfikar Ali Bhutto's government and had split from the Pakistan People's Party soon after Zia ul-Haq's coup d'état in 1977. He was in the political wilderness at the time he wrote the articles about Rushdie's book. The ISI did him a political favor by providing him an issue to revive his political fortunes. As for the ISI's motives, the agency was repeating what Pakistani intelligence services had successfully done in the past: It was hoping to embarrass an elected civilian government over an emotive religious issue and pave the way for the Benazir Bhutto government's dismissal in a palace coup.

After the publication of Kausar Niazi's articles in the Urdu press, another veteran of similar campaigns, Maulana Abdul Sattar Niazi, called a conference of ulema (Islamic religious scholars) to demand action against Rushdie. As a young man Sattar Niazi had been part of the campaign for Pakistan's creation. After independence, he had been part of almost every religious-political campaign that helped the military's intervention in politics, starting with the anti-Ahmedi protests of 1953. The government had already banned *Satanic Verses,* and officials in Bhutto's administration did not know what else to do in response to the ulema's fresh campaign.[32] For their part, the Islamist organizers of the anti-Rushdie protests took the position that the publication of the book was an American-Zionist conspiracy against Islam.

On February 12, 1989, two days before Ayatollah Khomeini issued his fatwa, the two Niazis led a protest of about eight thousand young male demonstrators in Islamabad outside the American Center, a United States government information office. At the end of the day, the Pakistani government declared that the publishers of the book, Viking Penguin, had to destroy all copies of it. If this directive was not followed, all books published by Viking Penguin would be proscribed. Indicative of the unqualified rage against Rushdie at the time was the fact that *The Satanic Verses,* as of that date, had not been translated into Urdu, had not been distributed in Pakistan, was banned from sale in Pakistan, and, consequently, had not been read in Pakistan.

During the demonstration led by the two Niazis, protesters attacked the U.S. Information Service building. They carried signs that read, "America and Israel: Enemies of Islam."[33] Police had to shoot at the mob to disperse demonstrators and protect the lives of Pakistanis and Americans inside in the building. Five demonstrators were killed.[34] The news of the violent Pakistani protests drew international attention to Rushdie's book and probably led to Ayatollah Khomeini's fatwa against the author as a blasphemer. The Ayatollah is unlikely to have read the book on his own. In Pakistan, it exacerbated the religious parties' hatred of Bhutto and her fledgling pro-Western administration. Rushdie's American publishers had earlier published Bhutto's autobiography *Daughter of the East,* enabling her detractors to link the two, however tenuous that connection.[35] The storming of the U.S. Information Service in the presence of CNN cameras brought images of the burning of American flags in Benazir Bhutto's Pakistan into U.S. homes, undermining Bhutto's credentials as America's friend. The ISI managed to keep its role in the affair hidden. Rushdie has continued to be vilified in Pakistan unabated.

In *Shame,* Rushdie writes, "I build imaginary countries and try to impose them on the ones that exist."[36] Although Rushdie has explained that *Midnight's Children* should not be viewed as the "India book" and *Shame* as the "Pakistan book," many literary critics and academics have been unable to resist such a reading. But it cannot be denied that the primary subject of *Shame* is Pakistan and its ruling elite as well as an exploration of the origins of Pakistan. He writes, "It is well known that the term 'Pakistan,' an acronym, was originally thought up in England by a group of Muslim intellectuals. P for the Punjabis, A for the Afghans, K for the Kashmiris, S for Sind and the 'tan,' they say, for Baluchistan." The creation of Pakistan is, to Rushdie, "an unnatural birth."[37] Talking of *Shame,* he says, "Whether or not it is desirable or undesirable that Pakistan should exist is really a question that the book doesn't discuss. If you ask me, I don't think Pakistan has a long-term chance of surviving."[38]

As a Pakistani born well after partition, and who has known no other homeland, I understand and even sympathize with Rushdie's critique of Pakistan. But I am unable to dispense with the idea of home, and millions like me now know only Pakistan as their only domicile. Pakistan's median age today is nineteen, which means that 75 million of its 150 million inhabitants are less than nineteen years old and have not seen either the 1947 partition of India or the 1971 separation of Bangladesh. For the sake of these young Pakistanis, a reimagining of Pakistan is needed, going beyond the bitterness of the 1947 partition and the disasters inflicted upon Pakistanis by their own rulers and leaders.

One can be agnostic about whether the creation of the state of Pakistan in August 1947 was a tragedy or not. But there is no doubt that the failure of Pakistanis to create a more tolerant and democratic state and the difficult reconciliation between India and Pakistan have been catastrophic. Ever since their nation's creation, Pakistanis have felt compelled to defend their nationhood and to constantly define and redefine their identity. This identity crisis can be likened to the psychosis of the unwanted child who is informed at an early age that his birth was unplanned, unwanted, or an accident—or, even worse, a mistake.

Another metaphor for partition can be that of a bitter divorce. The party that did not want the divorce (India) is unable to forgive the party that walked out (Pakistan). Pakistan remains insecure as a result of its treatment by India after the divorce. A custody battle (the unresolved dispute over Kashmir) ensues, as both parties are unable to communicate with each other without lapsing into an endless debate about the circumstances surrounding the divorce itself.

Pakistan's unfortunate history justifies Rushdie's description of Pakistan as "insufficiently imagined," but imagination is by definition not a finite process. An entity that is insufficiently imagined can be reimagined. Just as the imagination "can falsify, demean, ridicule, caricature and wound," it can also serve to "clarify, intensify and unveil."[39] Many Pakistanis are working, albeit with great difficulty, to reimagine Pakistan as Rushdie would—as an inclusive, pluralist, democratic, modern state that works toward the well-being of its own people, instead of being preoccupied with endlessly defining itself, especially in relation to India. As Rushdie writes in *Imaginary Homelands,* imagination "is the process by which we make pictures of the world" and "is one of the keys to our humanity."[40] Perhaps some day that process of reimagining Pakistan will result in a more positive picture.

NOTES

The opening epigraph is from Pradyumma S. Chauhan, ed., *Salman Rushdie Interviews: A Sourcebook of His Ideas* (Connecticut: Greenwood Press, 2001), 77.

1. Salman Rushdie, *Imaginary Homelands: Essays and Criticism, 1981–1991* (London: Granta Books, 1991), 27.

2. Chauhan, *Salman Rushdie Interviews,* 66.

3. Rushdie, *Imaginary Homelands,* 53.

4. Rushdie, *Imaginary Homelands,* 55.

5. Chauhan, *Salman Rushdie Interviews* p 65.

6. Rushdie, *Imaginary Homelands,* 58.

7. Rushdie, *Imaginary Homelands,* 10.

8. Rushdie, *Imaginary Homelands,* 9.

9. Salman Rushdie, *Step across This Line: Collected Nonfiction, 1992–2002* (New York: Random House, 2002), 370.

10. Chauhan, *Salman Rushdie Interviews,* 10.

11. Rushdie, *Step across This Line,* 371.

12. For a discussion of the relatively weak support for Pakistan in the Pakistan areas, and the local politics behind it, see Ian Talbot, *Pakistan—a Modern History* (New York: St. Martin's Press, 1998), 66–94.

13. Dennis Kux, *The United States and Pakistan, 1947–2000: Disenchanted Allies* (Washington D.C.: Woodrow Wilson Center Press, 2001), 7. See also Ayesha Jalal, *The Sole Spokesman: Jinnah, the Muslim League, and the Demand for Pakistan* (Cambridge: Cambridge University Press, 1985).

14. Ayesha Jalal, *The State of Martial Rule* (Cambridge: Cambridge University Press, 1990), 16.

15. Jalal, *State of Martial Rule,* 16–18.

16. Jalal, *State of Martial Rule,* 18.

17. Fortnightly Report to the Viceroy by Sir Evan Jenkins, Governor of Punjab, February 1947, British India Library, Records of the Political and Secret Department, L/P & J/5/250, p. 3/79.

18. Jinnah's conversation of May 1, 1947, with U.S. diplomat Raymond Hare, cited in Kux, *Disenchanted Allies,* 13.

19. Jalal, *State of Martial Rule,* 18.

20. Rushdie, *Imaginary Homelands,* 377.

21. Rushdie, *Step across This Line.*

22. Michael Reder, ed., *Conversations with Salman Rushdie* (Jackson: University Press of Mississippi, 2000), 217.

23. W. J. Weatherby, *Salman Rushdie: Sentenced to Death* (New York: Caroll and Graf Publishers, 1990).

24. Weatherby, *Salman Rushdie.*

25. Weatherby, *Salman Rushdie.*

26. Reder, *Conversations with Salman Rushdie,* 31.

27. Rushdie, *Imaginary Homelands,* 37–38.

28. Chauhan, *Salman Rushdie Interviews,* 67.

29. M. M. R. Khan, *The United Nations and Kashmir* (Groningen, Netherlands: J. B. Wolters, 1956), 62.

30. Salman Rushdie, *Shame.*

31. Author's conversation with Maulana Kausar Niazi, Islamabad, October 6, 1993.

32. Iqbal Akhund, *Trial and Error: The Advent and Eclipse of Benazir Bhutto* (Karachi: Oxford University Press, 2000), 59–60.

33. Richard M. Weintraub, "Mob Storms U.S. Facility in Pakistan: At Least Five Killed as Police Open Fire on Moslem Protesters," *Washington Post,* February 13, 1989.

34. Weintraub, "Mob Storms U.S. Facility."

35. Akhund, *Trial and Error,* 60.

36. Akhund, *Trial and Error,* 60.

37. Damian Grant, *Salman Rushdie* (Plymouth, UK: Northcote House, 1999).

38. Grant, *Salman Rushdie.*

39. Rushdie, *Imaginary Homelands,* 143.

40. Rushdie, *Imaginary Homelands,* 143.

THOMAS BLOM HANSEN

Reflections on Salman Rushdie's Bombay

In his well-known essay *Imaginary Homelands* Salman Rushdie writes: "Bombay is a city built by foreigners upon reclaimed land." A few lines later he adds that "it is entirely Indian in spirit and sentiment." *Midnight's Children* was created out of a desire to remember and re-create the author's own childhood in this environment where the familiar and intimate constantly intersected with unfamiliar, if not utterly alien, universes of language, habits, and conduct. Rushdie writes: "I realised how much I wanted to restore the past to myself, not in the faded greys of old family albums, but whole, in Cinemascope and glorious Technicolor."

The tale of Saleem Sinai, the narrator in the novel, is a high-octane, often hilarious story set in a Bombay that trickles through the book in bits and fragmented images as seen through the eyes of the narrator. A story unfolding in Bombay, though not a story about Bombay, Saleem's tale is nonetheless emblematic of the metropolis's place in modern India. A city built and developed by foreigners, India's foremost bridgehead to the world, throughout the twentieth century its most modern and commercial city, the origin of the Bollywood film industry—and like that industry regarded as glamorous and excessive, but also deeply amoral and flawed. Like the city, Saleem is impure and inauthentic in every respect—the result of an illicit affair between a departing Englishman and a woman of low birth. Baby Saleem is born at the same time as a son born to the wealthy Sinai family. To please her radical boyfriend, the maid of the Sinai family decides to swap the babies. Saleem grows up as a Sinai in the elite Malabar Hill area, where his large nose is taken as proof of his Kashmiri genes. The nose is more poignantly a sign of his quintessential mongrelized Bombay-ness and his affinity with the city's favorite god, the wise elephant-headed Ganesh, whose pedigree also is somewhat unclear. The biological son of the Sinai family is placed in the cot of a poor musician's wife, and grows up in the streets of Bombay to become Shiva, a tough and violent kid. This pair, Saleem and Shiva, embodies Rushdie's idea of Bombay: Equally impure in origin, Saleem is wise, idealist, and fragile, and Shiva, violent, amoral, and robust. They combine the high and the low, the elegant western side of the city with its underside and its bow-els—the teeming slums and vast industrial areas and chawls in its central and eastern sectors.

This duality and the celebration of the openness of the city, its cosmopolitanism and intense mix of people, languages, pedigrees, and prejudices is at the heart of Saleem's childhood Bombay. Rushdie remarks somewhere that the hit song of the late 1950s "Mera Joota hai Japani" (My boots are Japanese) could have been Saleem's theme song, not least because its last line says "dil hai Hindustani," my heart is Indian.

Rushdie strongly believes in what he calls "the non-sectarian philosophy" that was the basis of modern India and that had unique resonance in the overflowing diversity and go-getting atmosphere of Bombay. *Midnight's Children* is, as Rushdie asserts, fundamentally an optimistic book that hints at what he calls the "infinite possibilities of the country."

That optimistic tone had changed when *The Moor's Last Sigh* was published in 1995. The style is rich, idiosyncratic, and humorous as ever but the tone is darker and more cynical, not least in the middle section set in Bombay. The book is in many ways a meditation on the demise of the older elite ideals of a secular and tolerant India in the face of the rise of a new, violent, and bigoted form of Hindu nationalist politics. The view of Bombay foregrounds the intimate intermingling and interdependence of the city's social worlds, but the encounters between these worlds, and the elite's essential dependence on murky transactions and the underworld are depicted as hypocritically disavowed, morally corrupt, and excessively violent. The protagonist is a boy whose body and physique develops much faster than his mind—maybe a metaphor for the city, for India, or for the "out-of-jointness" of the elite family he is born into? His mother is a modernist painter, and every year when Ganesh is celebrated in huge public processions, she dances in her colorful dress on the top of her house in Malabar Hill, displaying her rebellious contempt for what she regards as a primitive mass festival unfolding at the beach deep below her. The immature and uncontrolled strength of the man-child who becomes known as the "Moor" finds a temporary home and soul mates among the violent followers of Mumbai Axis, a movement and gangster organization led by the dubious figure Raman Fielding—an obvious mockery of Bal Thackeray, the leader of Shiv Sena, the violent and chauvinistic party that has been a powerful and at times dominant factor in the life of the city and the state of Maharashtra since the late 1960s. Shiv Sena started as a populist organization defending the interests of the local Marathi population and became famous for it many local branches across the city that assisted ordinary people in getting jobs, housing, and amenities.[1] The organization also acquired fame and notoriety for its systematic use of violence against those it in various periods have considered "aliens"—South Indians, Communists, Muslims, and so on. Thackeray, whose violent anti-Muslim and antiminority rhetoric is fully matched by a boundless vanity, banned Rushdie's book from Bombay for several years. The same fate befell the film *Bombay,* directed by the highly acclaimed director Mani Ratnam, mainly because it portrayed a militant Hindu leader modeled on Thackeray as an ugly man with buck teeth!

There is a sliding in tone and perspective in Rushdie's depiction of Bombay: first the familiar, bubbly, confused but also rich and encompassing Bombay of Saleem Sinai's childhood in the 1950s, and later the more brutal, unforgiving and corrupted Bombay depicted in *The Moor's Last Sigh (MLS),* the Bombay that in fact became Mumbai the same year. This marked "the birth of a new India, when money, as well as religion, was breaking all shackles on its desires" (*MLS,* 344). What Rushdie refers to is of course the concomitant rise of Hindu nationalism and a new unshackled capitalist economy in India in the 1990s. What I find most gratifying in *The Moor's Last Sigh* is that Rushdie never tries to reduce this transformation to the effects of the work of evil forces like Mumbai Axis, although Fielding and his violent disciples are depicted in a far from flattering light. By letting the protagonist Moor become part of this milieu suffused with violence, Rushdie affords us a somewhat more empathetic glimpse of its ethos of "virile pleasures of comradeship and all-for-one." By letting his father Abraham work hand in glove with the underworld, Rushdie also makes it clear that the greed and vanity of the country's older so-called secular elite were, and remain, deeply involved in the making of the new "god-and-mammon India" (*MLS,* 351).

In hindsight there was a strong sense of premonition of this transformation of the city in Rushdie's book, a premonition I strongly felt along with the millions of others who like me experienced the riots and violence in Bombay in that fateful winter of 1992–93. Rushdie's fiction thus resonates deeply with the experience of change in the city and the feeling that the Bombay of old, or the Bombay *classique* of the 1950s and 1960s, is irrevocably lost. The innocence and the optimism of postcolonial Bombay that played such a crucial role in Bollywood's depiction of the new nation and its futures is today definitely a thing of the past. That Bombay of modernist dreams, the *swapaneer nagari,* has given way to another set of dreams, dreamed by people other than those who filled the universe of *Midnight's Children.* Initially I wanted to call my book on the city "Mumbai Dreams" because I thought it captured this important shift in how Bombay was constructed as a utopian space, but my publisher was worried that no Americans would understand the name Mumbai. My Indian friends told me that the book would sound like a novel by Shobha De, the Indian equivalent of Joan Collins! I decided that it was a no-win situation and went for another title.[2] But the fact remains that the idea of Bombay and the connotations that name carried, have given way to another idea of the city, other connotations, and therefore also another idea of India.

In order to shed some light on this change that Rushdie captures so precisely, I need to step into a more familiar role as a social scientist and explore some of the ambiguities and socio-cultural tensions that have shaped the history of what for many people always will remain Bombay, regardless of its recent change of name.

The Idea of Bombay

Let me return to the "idea" of Bombay. How can a city be an idea, and how can a mongrelize city that literally is built by foreigners on an island and surrounding marshland off the coast become a powerful symbol of an entire nation, one may ask?

The answer lies in the fact that the idea of Bombay always was much bigger and more powerful than the city itself because it represented modernity, and importantly, an Indian modernity.

In a wonderful paper on Bombay, Gyan Prakash, who grew up in the northern state of Bihar, reflects on how crucial Bombay was to ideas of what modernity meant in this rather remote rural part of India. He writes: "We had heard of New York, Paris and London but they were foreign exotic places with no emotional resonance for us. Bombay on the other hand was our own, a part of India."[3]

Prakash explains how the Hindi cinema introduced him to the latest new fashion. I should add that into the essential mongrel tongue of the streets of Bombay, *Bambaiya boli,* the word *latest* has become entirely incorporated, now pronounced "ladest"—meaning modern and up there. For Prakash and millions like him, the style and bodily comportment of actors on the screen, and of his relatives living in the distant city, seemed to transmit self-confidence, individuality, and independence—the very ideal of the modern human being.

The Parsis—the light-skinned people who had fled persecution in Persia and had come to India a millennium ago—were seen as the quintessential Bombayites. They were not from India, but indeed of

India and were in many respects the pioneers in developing an Indian modernity, and certainly an Indian capitalism. In the nineteenth century, Bombay became a major center of shipbuilding, textiles, and engineering. British capital played a role, and Bombay's entrepreneurs and ship magnates were from many communities, not least Gujaratis, but the Parsis dominated both in business and in the modern professions, as lawyers and as administrators. The Parsis formed the core of what was, in the nineteenth century, the first non-Western and non-white industrial bourgeoisie in the world, and in the first decades of the twentieth century Bombay was one of the foremost centers of industrial production outside the West. Parsis, such as the legendary Tata family, seemed to embody the virtues of modernity as they were represented within the empire—individualistic, daring, self-made, thoroughly anglicized, but also civil and law abiding in their conduct. Parsis were, and aspired to be, the darlings of empire and the most loyal supporters of British rule. They later became heroes of the postcolonial nation because of their effortless command of business, law, and the modern city of Bombay they had built.

Trading communities from Gujarat, both Hindus and Muslims, also played a crucial role in the city's development. Bombay was, and remains, in fact an important center for Gujarati culture and economic networks. During the turmoils of the 1950s, when a powerful linguistic movement among Marathi speakers demanded a separate state, Bombay's identity as either Gujarati or Marathi was at stake. In spite of some violence against the Gujarati middle class at the time, it is noteworthy that Gujaratis, who literally own most of the city, never have been singled out as "aliens" or threatening others. Gujaratis, if mostly the Hindus among them, are generally accepted and in fact admired by many Maharashtrians for their enterprising spirit and modernity.

This classical Bombay with its elegant streets, squares, and houses also had its dark sides, and they have many been richly represented in the Hindi cinema over the decades. The idea of the city as a mechanical place, full of noise and instrumentalized social relations, was widespread in films and books. The huge working class lived in chawls and slums, where life was a struggle and landlords and employers were harsh. The city also became home to a strong and legendary trade union movement—the *lalbhais,* the red brothers. The idea of Bombay's corruption of the soul and the body—its criminals, its underworld, prostitution, and gambling was, and remains, another rich vein tapped in cinema, in novels, and in journalism. No other urban space in India was, or is to this day, so suggestive, exciting, and titillating as that of Bombay.

So strong was this image of Bombay as the quintessential modern city structured by modern and rational forces of industry, law, and bureaucracy that other processes and forces almost disappeared from academic and official analysis. Most academic work done on twentieth-century Bombay has been done by historians of labor and industry. It has been the conviction of many Indian academics until a decade ago that Bombay because of its modern character was less prone to sectarian violence. The recurrent riots in the city from the 1890s, in the 1920s, 1946, and in the 1960s and 1970s were usually explained in terms of class, as essentially economic conflicts not driven by irrationalities anchored in religious bigotry, caste sentiments, and the other ailments that the nationalist elite associated with traditional and not-yet-modernized India.

Today, after the collapse of the classical Bombay, we realize that there were other forces at work. Indian social scientists also recognize that there is nothing particularly "traditional" about sectarian violence. In fact, the conflicts and continued production of deadly stereotypes between Hindus and Muslims is at the very heart of the experience of modern, urban India, and at the heart of the subcontinent's colonial and postcolonial history. The latest pogroms in Gujarat in 2002 suggest that today there is hardly even any effort made—as in the past—to conceal the political expediency and semiofficial nature of this ritualized politics of death.

It is a commonplace observation in linguistics that the last word in a sentence determines the meaning of the entire sentence. In the winter 1992–93, Bombay was rocked by the worst riots ever, a veritable anti-Muslim pogrom that left almost a thousand people dead and many more wounded and homeless. Shiv Sena was the main responsible force behind the killings and went on to win the state elections in 1995, riding on the back of the most poisonous political rhetoric ever deployed in India. This forced many to revise their ideas of what forces and sentiments really drove Bombay's public life underneath its surface of civility and commercial dynamism.

The Beast in the Belly

If one asks an average person in Mumbai about the riots of 1992–93 the reply will invariably be that it was the work of criminal forces and some corrupt politicians. One will hear that ordinary people have no problems with each other and that they just want to get on with their lives.

Today, some might even add that it all was provoked by terrorists, Muslim terrorists. It is tempting to accept this explanation especially because politicians indeed were involved, so were criminal figures, and it is equally true that one finds moving stories of neighborliness and humanity in the midst of an incredibly poisoned atmosphere of death and revenge. But there was more to the riots, much more, as anyone who experienced the riots and the uncannily silent and ominous atmosphere that engulfed the city for almost two weeks will know. Most people I met before, during, and after the riots were emotionally deeply involved in them, and many Hindus, probably a majority, fully supported Shiv Sena in their self-professed goal of "teaching the Muslims a lesson." I spent several days moving around in the city during the riots relying on terrified taxi drivers who nonetheless saw me, the *gora,* as a guarantee of their own safety. The men who stood along the roads and on rooftops with iron bars, kerosene bottles, and long knives and engaged in battles with "the other community" were neither criminals nor bad characters from the *zopadpattis,* the slums, as the dominant middle-class imagination will hold. They were family men from all walks of life—filled with anxiety, with hatred, but they were also excited and upbeat about this collective transgression of all rules of civility—of killing, burning, and looting.

It was as if a whole layer of moderation, civility, and cautious public speech had been removed and instead ethno-religious hatred had emerged in a rather naked form. Its dominant form was a strange mortal fear of an imagined Muslim menace projected onto the limited and impoverished Muslim minority in the city. Its outward manifestation was a self-righteous—and therefore murderous—feeling of victimization and an entitlement to defend oneself and one's own family and community against this allegedly ubiquitous but elusive and ill-defined threat.

Like many others, I asked myself why the civility and capacity of coexistence once attributed to Bombay disappeared so suddenly. Was it always just a fiction, an idea rather than a practice? Or was it merely a public code of conduct that had concealed more unforgiving and xenophobic attitudes that for long had existed within homes, and within the various linguistic and social worlds in the city? Let me briefly outline the anatomy of fear and aggression that seems to have changed Bombay irreversibly. In order to do so we need to follow Rushdie and step out of the elite and middle-class imaginings of order, law, and predictability and instead delve into some of the many parallel universes that always defined Bombay. I will limit myself to two interlinked universes—the world of Shiv Sena and the underworld—both of them real and embodied but also suffused with fantasy and spectral beings.

The Sovereignty of Excess

There has always been a wide range of activities in Indian cities that could be characterized as semilegal or illegal. But the line between illegality and legality is anything but self-evident and is often irrelevant. As anyone familiar with the organization of social life in popular neighborhoods in India will know, local fixers, and men of local eminence who broke contacts between ordinary people and authorities, and extend help of various sorts, have always been of crucial importance in the networks of dependency, exploitation, and debt that organize life in slums and chawls. These men have always been paid in cash or kind. They have been able to organize protection of residents, while others have extorted money on a regular basis. They have also been money lenders, patrons of religious festivals, donating money to orphanages, education, and political parties, settling local disputes, and so on. Such a local figure of eminence is known as a *bhai* (brother), or if more established as a *dada* (lit. grandfather, often used for elder brother as well). Such men, *dade,* are seen as a sort of indispensable parasites within local moral parameters, both loathed and respected. Ubiquitous, informal, and impossible to fix within the parameters of formal law, these men and their networks constitute elementary units of governance, of political parties as well as the administration of justice in popular urban neighborhoods. They embody the opacity of urban life, and some of them, or parts of their activities, also form elementary units in what are termed "criminal rackets," or gangs, of slumlords, bootleggers, extortionists, and smugglers.

The most profound change in Bombay in the last decade is that these men have become far more visible and assertive than in the 1950s of Saleem Sinai's childhood. Decades of democracy—unruly and often unwieldy—have enabled a new breed of public figures to make their way into politics using powerful populist rhetoric. During the Nehruvian period the ideal of public speech and appearance was that of the cultured and reasonable gentleman, but since the 1970s a more coarse, plebeian, but also heroic type has appeared: the self-made man whose reputation in the slums and popular neighborhoods often is based on his capacity for violence, his underworld connections, and his gang of young men ready to help his friends and terrorize his enemies. This process, and the inability of the state to arrest and prosecute Bal Thackeray for his obvious incitement of violence over several decades, revealed that the writ of the law was rather less impressive than imagined by many citizens. Was this only due to deep and endemic corruption at all levels, as it so often explained in public debates on the "criminalization of politics" in contemporary India? Or was this revealing, more disturbingly, that the entire juridical edifice of the postcolonial state was built on foundations that were rather shaky and fragmented? Not unlike the city itself, perhaps, built on drained marshland, but in constant need of support and maintenance by ingenuous systems—like the concrete tripods developed by Saleem Sinai's father in *Midnight's Children*. Does it mean that the state's monopoly of violence always was illusory and that the de facto right and capacity to kill, punish, and discipline with impunity was distributed among a range of forces in the city, and in modern India? I believe this to be the case.[4] The formation of the colonial state from the eighteenth century onward in India took place in a land with a complex array of systems of governance, laws, and authority. Gradually the British established their supremacy through warfare, alliances, and the language of the law presented to Indian subjects as Britain's gift of civilization to the subcontinent. Yet, for all its aspirations and pretensions, the writ of the law was established through a systematic application of excessive force. Public gallows were introduced and colonial courts used the death penalty with far greater frequency than indigenous courts (Singha 1998). For all its efforts and use of force, the rule of law depended on indirect rule, and on a systematic distinction between those subjects with property and education who enjoyed the protection of the law—but never the near-impunity that was extended to high-ranking Englishmen—and the overwhelming majority, the great unwashed, who were governed through intermediaries, headmen and local leaders often invested with authority by colonial officers. The new state of midnight's children established universal franchise and extended formal legal protection to all, but these basic structures of power, the dispersal of authority and the right to use violence, were not changed.

Instead, as democracy deepened, the poor became more restless and assertive and began looking for leaders who spoke like them, who were of the popular world and who knew how to use the crowd—always the specter haunting colonial officials—to the maximum effect. Populist leaders could now carve out a space of autonomy and impunity based on the numerical and therefore electoral strength of the popular world, and the fear it engendered among the middle classes. The actions, the bodily comportment, the lifestyle and utterances of these men—defiant and excessive in both violence and consumption—

became the very symbol of a new and enticing sense of freedom and recognition, however flimsy. This amounted to a certain dispersal of sovereignty, a displacement of authority and the use of violence from the paternalist state and the nationalist-secular elite to less lofty and more ambiguous wielders of power. Such a de facto "democratization of violence" is a powerful theme in *The Moor's Last Sigh*. Rushdie clearly recognizes that democracy have released more elementary and ambiguous forces and desires:

> There was a thing that Raman Fielding knew, which was his power's secret source: that it is not the civil social norm for which men yearn, but the outrageous, the outsize, the out-of-bounds—for that by which our wild potency may be unleashed. We crave permission openly to become our secret selves. (305)

Rushdie captures so precisely how the Shiv Sena and the mythical underworld signifies the rise of a new public ethos of freedom through excess. The multiple little "big men" in the city felt increasingly liberated to flaunt their often illegitimate wealth, to brutalize their opponents, and to indulge in all kinds of pleasures.

Let me briefly turn to Georges Bataille to understand this phenomenon. To Bataille sovereignty is not merely an archaic form of power but is a force articulated more fundamentally in human life in attitudes, or acts, beyond the realm of utility and calculation. "Life beyond utility is the domain of sovereignty" (Bataille 1991, 198).[5] A sovereign command does not calculate minutely what it wants, but inadvertently reproduces obedience *qua* its very gesture of disregard of danger and death (225–30). Sovereignty resides in every human being and shows itself in the desire to enjoy and revel in brief moments of careless freedom, in sexual ecstasy, in moments of simple nonanticipatory existence, when an individual experiences "the miraculous sensation of having the world at his disposal" (199). This was the original condition of man in "his non-alienated condition . . . but what is within him has a destructive violence, for example the violence of death" (214).

The essence of Bataille's proposition is that because the exercise of sovereignty is linked to death, excessive expenditure *(depenser)* and bodily pleasure can neither be contained by any discipline, nor be fully "democratized" into an equal dignity of all men. Because sovereignty revolves around death, the ultimate form of expenditure beyond utility, it constitutes, in Mbembe's words, an "anti-economy (Mbembe 2003, 15).

To Bataille, sovereignty has no positive existence but is a miracle intrinsic to human existence and can only be determined through what he calls a "negative theology" that captures the "miraculous moments" (241) where sovereignty is experienced: in the awe of the leader or the king, in the disregard of death, of timidity, of prohibitions. Because sovereignty flows from the assertion of a basic life force that foregrounds the body and the senses rather than the intellect, it is ultimately connected with the will to take life, and to give up one's life but not in a calculated and rational fashion. Sovereignty is the opposite of "faint-heartedness," and Bataille writes: "Killing is not the only way to regain sovereign life, but sovereignty is always linked to a denial of the sentiments that death controls" (221).

The somewhat complacent vision of law and civility based on rigid and unquestioned barriers of class, hierarchy, and caste that characterized the colonial city of Bombay has given way to a more accessible, egalitarian, but also much more brutal vision of life, based on excess, violence, and on the de facto sovereignty of the self-made man.

Shiv Sena and Cultural Intimacy

The style and methods of Shiv Sena and the rhetoric of its leader Bal Thackeray are all in some ways marked by excess. Excessive xenophobia, excessive violence, excessive corruption, flamboyancy. But it is also marked by a sense of cultural intimacy, of promoting the well-known, the ordinary, colloquial, vernacular, and unsophisticated world of the ordinary Maharashtrian. For years the movement was seen as a curiosity, something marginal and uncouth that could not be taken seriously by intellectuals and the cultural elite in the city. Meanwhile, the movement built up its strength and its networks in popular neighborhoods where it provided a home to ambitious local businesspeople, local strongman types, and to thousands of young men who felt marginalized in the city, but empowered by the rhetoric and ethnic solidarity promoted by the Sena. What was overlooked by many so-called secular people was that Shiv Sena deftly tapped the uneasiness with urban life, and the alienation many ordinary Marathi speakers felt in a city so dominated by sophisticated anglicized Parsis and by Gujarati businessmen—Muslims and Hindu. This alienation had deep roots in the region's history and in the linguistic movement of the 1950s. Shiv Sena's bids to claim and mark the physical spaces of the city—from the promotion of the Ganapati festival, its vow to rename the city after the local goddess Mumbadevi worshipped by the original fishermen of the marshland, and its resolve to"'cleanse" the city of undesirable elements—Muslims, criminals, militant untouchables, and so forth—won it broad support also in the respectable middle-class milieus where it had its political and cultural roots. Shiv Sena came to dominate Bombay in the 1980s and 1990s until ousted by voters in 2000 because of its incompetence, corruption, and misrule. The movement is still alive and kicking, and it has probably changed Bombay more than even the premonitions of Rushdie indicated.

Shiv Sena is also a symptom of a broader trend in business and political life in India that indeed has made the playing field more open but also more merciless and exploitative. Just as the Mumbai Axis in the *Moor's Last Sigh* depended on patronage from powerful tycoons and the corrupted elite, so has Shiv Sena since its inception depended on protection by the police, and by powerful forces at the heart of Bombay's business establishment. However, when Shiv Sena arrived at the power and the public recognition they so desired in 1995 they actually did not know what to do with it—except to enjoy it, to live the dream. In Bataille's view the enjoyment of the sovereign moment flows from a certain suspension of mores, of judgment, and of the reasonable self. There is in fact emptiness, a void, at the heart of sovereignty; something that cannot be sustained unless the gesture, or the violence, is repeated over and over. The dreams and desires that Shiv Sena always tapped into so effectively were always split between a desire to achieve respectability and social recognition, and a desire to rebel against strictures of convention in order to become manly, assertive, bold, and self-respecting—the state of mind of the ideal Sainik, or "warrior," for the Shiv Sena movement.

Shiv Sena's program was always vague and general, but neither the lack of a larger vision nor the difficulties in initiating and implementing structural reforms were unique to the Shiv Sena. What was unique was that no larger vision or consistent policy possibly could develop in Shiv Sena because of the specific style in which control was exercised by Thackeray over the movement. After a short period in power it became clear that the two driving motives of the Sena, respect and self-respect, were incompatible. They referred to different symbolic registers, and required different and often conflicting commands to the rank-and-file Sainiks. Manohar Joshi, as chief minister, became the ultimate symbol of Shiv Sena's quest for respectability and the ascendancy of its leadership into Mumbai's parvenu elite. Thackeray strove to retain his position as a law onto himself in order to retain his enormous authority in the party structure and hold he has on the imagination of millions of people in the state. He remained the producer, the authorizer, and the incarnation of the somewhat obstinate Sainik style of defiance of authority.

How can one understand the continued efficacy of Thackeray's style of openly irresponsible leadership, the longing for his unrelenting commands, the enjoyment of his idiosyncratic utterances among the many followers and admirers in Mumbai? Let us turn to Hegel's classical reflections on the relationship between master and slave.

In Alexander Kojève's reading of Hegel's master-slave dialectic, what is desired by the slave is "the desire of the desire of the other," that is, the recognition *(annerkennung)* of his humanity, and thus his desirability, by the master. The slave asks the master to "see me as who I am," and constitutes his own identity through this confrontation with the other. In Kojève's dramatic and teleological reading the slaves, that is, the ordinary human beings, move history and are the truly creative figures through their tremendous drive toward recognition and freedom. The masters (the elites, the aristocracy), on their side, are doomed as they have nothing to strive for: the recognition they strive for may be easily given but is worthless because it is given by slaves and only reproduces the master as what he already is (Kojève 1969, 45–55).

As it has been pointed out by Lacan, this compelling logic of identity is always incomplete. If the subject is born in the encounter with the desire of the other, its identity depends on the character of this desire, that is, the gaze of the other—here understood as what Lacan terms the symbolic order: authorities, dominant discourses, social conventions, and so on. This gaze, the other's desire, cannot be fully fathomed and understood, and the subject is therefore bound to be a subject of radical doubt and uncertainty. Žižek argues that this uncertainty defines the subject and suspends it between an anxiety and desire. "Anxiety is aroused by the desire of the Other in the sense that 'I do not know what *objet a*[6] I am for the desire of the other.' What does the Other want from me, what is there—in me more than myself—on account of which I am the object of desire of the Other" (Žižek 1997, 71).

What is posed to the other is therefore not "see me for what I am" (because I cannot know) but rather the probing and anxious question, *Ché vuoi?* "What do you see in me?"

Subjectivity is bound to take shape in this gaze, or desire, that cannot be fully fathomed, and the answer to this dilemma is what Žižek terms "anticipatory identification"—that we become what we think we are in eyes of the other. Instead of waiting anxiously for a symbolic mandate to arrive, to be hailed and thus become subject, as Althusser would have had it, human beings often anticipate the signs by which they are known to, and desired by, the other.

> Anticipatory identification is therefore a kind of pre-emptive strike, an attempt to provide in advance an answer to "what I am for the Other" and thus to assuage the anxiety that pertains to the desire of the Other. (Žižek 1997, 76)

The Shiv Sainiks are indeed haunted by the anxiety of fathoming what respectable society and the "establishment" sees in them—the ordinary men from a social world marked by the stain of the slums, the *zopad-pattis*. Is it contempt, respect or fear? The Sainik is bound to be split between, on the one hand, the gaze of respectable society that expects him to behave in accordance with established rules and conventions now that he has become part of that establishment, and, on the other hand, the gaze of the *Senapati,* the supreme leader. Thackeray does not expect conformity with established rules norms and conventions, but commands Sainiks to be self-respecting and assertive, but at the same time to obey his leadership unconditionally. He, by his example and rhetoric, is the one who affords them their self-respect and courage. The Sainik is in other words subject to two different commanding gazes, two different symbolic registers, and therefore also two different "anticipatory identifications": one is to become respectable, to indulge in enjoyment *(maza)* of one's newfound status, and to play by the rules; the other is to remain angry and continue to display courage *(sahas)* and manliness and to be in opposition.

But the latter is a precondition of the former. Sainiks have arrived in power and only command a measure of respect because of their aggressive attitude and forthrightness—in brief their plebeian *dada* style— through which they display their loyalty to Thackeray by anticipating what he sees in them. As a local Sena leader told me, "Without the Shiv Sena I am nobody."

Thackeray is the demanding father who expects loyalty and submission, who rules through the anxiety that his gaze and presence instills in Sainiks, especially the intermediate leaders who constantly are left doubting and asking themselves, "What does he see in me?" Yet by asserting his independence and the capacity for violence he commands through the loyalty of his Sainiks, he offers them a sense of freedom, of sovereignty, and a space of recognition within more established institutions. The anticipatory identification of Sainiks—in offices, in the streets, and elsewhere—is exactly to act as plebeians in the eyes of "the establishment," and thus to fill the role they have already been assigned. Because of their association with Shiv Sena they can self-consciously, and with self-respect, and with a measure of enjoyment of their own "nuisance value" wear the stain of the *zopadpatti*—the unpredictability and the threat of violence—which defines them and cannot be removed.

This stain of dirt and violence is also the cause of the desire and fascination of Shiv Sena by respectable middle-class society, the *objet petit a*—the sign of the unrepresentable Real—around which the identity as a Sainik is always/already organized in anticipation regardless of whether he actually has ever lived in a slum or ever carried out a violent act.

At the face of it Shiv Sena promises freedom, enjoyment, and self-respect to the ordinary Maharashtrian. Through his oratory and style, Thackeray celebrates urban modernity, Mumbai's modernity, and promises young men that to be a Sainik is to become a modern urban subject: the impatient, mobile young man who has no time for pompous leaders, slow bureaucrats, and self-important intellectuals. A Sainik is, and will always remain, wild at heart. Thackeray styles himself as the perfect example of the sovereign man, someone who is feared and respected because of his guts and disregard of danger.

However, the Sainik's sense of freedom and self-respect is illusory. His self-respect is tenuous, only attained through submission to the paternal and unpredictable law of Thackeray. The rebelliousness of the Sainiks never subverted moral and social conventions. Thackeray remains in many ways the traditional master commanding total and abiding loyalty. Shiv Sena does not want to transform society. Sainiks and their leaders merely want to muscle their way into respectable society through violence and the threat thereof. The truth of Thackeray's power is not that he is respected because of his guts, inventiveness, or personal courage, but because he has got many thousand loyal followers and an assumed capacity to create havoc in the city. He has repeatedly demonstrated his will to actually let his Sainiks loose on what he regards as enemies of the people, and in more recent times intellectuals, newspapers, and writers. However, the Sena has hardly ever confronted the state or any established center of power. The violence of Sainiks is exactly anticipatory identification—attempts to become real Sainiks, like fire, through violence. The violence of Sainiks does not grow out of desperation or poverty, but out of the command of Thackeray to let go of restrictions and social conventions, to act out frustrations and desires without bounds. Rushdie captures the attraction of this violent milieu when the Moor, while beating up the workers in textile district on behalf of Mainduck, reflects: "We crave permission to openly become our secret selves. . . . I found for the first time in my short-long life, the feeling of normality, of being nothing special, the sense of being among kindred spirits, among people-like-me, that is the defining quality of home" (*MLS,* 305).

Spectral Violence and the Figure of the Criminal

Judging from my own experiences and many conversations with people in Bombay over the years, the city is indeed not regarded as a dangerous place at the level of everyday experiences. Few people hesitate to walk the streets or sit alone on a train in the evening hours, homes are not fortified by burglar bars, and so on. The anxieties that produce the sense of danger, or more precisely, absence of safety, seem to be of a more intangible and abstract nature and relate more to the fundamental opacity and unknowability of the multilayered and varied life in the metropolis. In this respect there are remarkable continuities from the problems of knowledge and policing in colonial Bombay to those of contemporary Mumbai.

To colonial police officers the "hooligan" was the favored representation of this anonymous chaos, and in the postcolonial city the *badmash* (thug), especially the Muslim *badmash,* assumed a similar role as a relatively tangible representation of the frightening and fascinating chaos and anonymity, that is, the opacity around which the urban imaginary essentially is organized. In more recent times it was the hard core of the Muslim *badmash*—the hardened criminal, the mafia don— who became the ambivalent, frightening, but also ultimate symptom of Bombay's urban modernity. In the figure of the gangster is condensed and exaggerated all that is fascinating in urban existence: the effortless command over the complex urban landscape, hedonism, lavish consumption, fascination with technology, flashy clothes, classy women, ruthlessness, individuality, and so forth. All this makes the criminal deeply fascinating and, at the same time, an excessive figure of sovereign masculinity that is an antithesis to family values, decency, and civic norms. In other words, a perfect object to invoke in any discourse of order and discipline.

The alleged ubiquity of the underworld is, therefore, central to the claims of the police to be the defenders of society proper against chaos; it is posited as the central obstacle to creating a rational city according to city planners, claimed to be the underlying cause of communal riots, the cause of corruption and dishonesty in the world of politics, and so on.

It is unclear exactly when the term *gang* becomes the dominant concept through which police, officials, and the press tries to understand the hidden side of the city. However, in the 1970s a whole terminology and a set of narrative frames derived from the American gangster mythology became ever more popular in descriptions of Bombay's underworld. It became popular to look at the gang world as divided into four larger mafia-syndicates, each defined by a certain territory and headed by a don whose life story, lifestyle, and personal qualities through rumors and intensive press coverage became "talk of the town."

The most flamboyant of these characters was Haji Mastaan, a former coolie in the Bombay docks who through the 1970s had emerged as the king of contraband—cigarettes, cloth, electronic goods, gold. This hedonistic, chain-smoking man with artistic and spiritual inclinations—so the myth went—was never convicted. In the late 1970s he declared that he was reformed, turned to religion, and styled himself as a kind of godfather, affectionately known as Baba, an arbiter of conflicts among the new, more aggressive breed of young hotheads emerging in the early 1980s.

Karim Lala, the don of Dongri, wore the myth of the violent and shrewd Pathan with distinction, known by rumor and newspaper reports to specialize in extortion (a "typical" Pathan job) and *supari* (contract killing) as well as real estate. He was known as a staunch supporter of the Congress Party and admitted freely to the repeated embarrassment of political leaders that he donated money to the party coffers. Throughout his career, Lala cleverly played on his status as an incarnation of evil in the Marathi and Gujarati press. He obviously enjoyed the publicity and portrayed himself as a dignified, pious, and respectable citizen.

Vardharajan Mudaliar, the unassuming Tamil king of Dharavi and the vast South Indian colonies in Matunga and Sion, was another legendary figure. Colloquially known as Vardha, he made his money on illegal liquor, extortion, and smuggling. He was a major patron of temples, a keen supporter of non-Brahmin political and cultural organizations, and the man whose advice, protection, and opinion was sought by thousands of people. His modest home was known as the preferred informal court where disputes were settled and conflicts solved, and for decades he was said to be in a position to make and unmake political careers in his area. Vardha became the very model of a slumlord and gangster. Mani Rathnam's breakthrough film *Nayakan* (hero/star) from 1987 explicitly depicted Vardha's life and career through the narrative prism of the Corleone saga.

These dons did in a way incarnate all what respectable citizens of

Bombay would consider evil and dangerous—Muslims, slums, South Indian criminals. But it was also a somewhat familiar world where the evil forces were localized phenomena that did not have an impact on everyday life. This changed in 1983–84 when bloody rivalries between various "gangs" led to a series of highly publicized execution-style murders in public places, for instance of Shabir Ibrahim, brother of Dawood Ibrahim, the mythological gangster king of Mumbai. The killings were avenged in a highly dramatic style by a couple of daring contract killings in broad daylight in the Bombay High Court in front of the judge and police officers. This drama provided material for a series of popular writings and semifictionalized accounts of the romantic and dangerous world of the mafia. It also made the narrative frame of the mafia saga credible. As an editorial in a leading newspaper went: "Unless something drastic is done, Bombay will soon begin to resemble Chicago of the thirties and forties."[7]

These murders started a new era of more professional gangsterism and formation of new gangs armed with automatic weapons and cellular phones and dealing in drugs linked to international cartels. The legend of Dawood as a new, more brutal, more powerful, and more sophisticated type of underworld don was born and was only nurtured by the fact that Dawood moved to Dubai in 1985. From here Dawood controlled his growing empire, ranging from real estate, to film, drugs, and gambling, the police claimed. The standard picture of Dawood henceforth became that of the don dressed in flashy white playboy outfit, with sunglasses, on a boat or the racecourse, always with a cell phone in his hand. The quintessential gangster had become a part of the wealthy, high-tech-aided NRI (nonresident Indian) that emerged in the 1980s as the symbol of modernity and India's own backwardness.

The period after the Bhiwandi riots in 1984 also saw police officers, political leaders, and writers launch a powerful theory that communal riots were instigated by the (Muslim) mafia as a reaction against the actions of upright police officers or the bright light of investigative journalism (!) so loathed by the dons. A reporter wrote:

> The communal riots that rocked Bombay . . . brought into the open for the first time the tremendous reach and influence that the mafia dons had acquired over the years . . . the police crack down on the underworld last year brought the dons together . . . and a meeting of the four dons took place in March to map out a strategy. What followed a couple of months later was the worst ever riots to rock Bombay.[8]

This became a very popular theory that today can be heard all over the city. The reasons for its popularity are obvious: it invokes a scenario of conspiracy, a summit of evil forces as the cause of riots; it conveniently excludes the hazy world of politics, removes the heavy hand of Hindu nationalist organizations in instigating the violence, puts the blame squarely on the Muslim *badmash;* it exonerates the police force and thus produces a fantasy of the city as "almost normal" except for the "cancer" of the Muslim underworld that produces these unintelligible outburst of chaos and violence. Again, the "hardened criminal" is the somewhat empty signifier that makes the opacity of the urban landscape intelligible.

Where Now, Mumbai?

Of late, it is said, Bombay/Mumbai has lost some of it attraction. Bombay was the center of classical industrial capitalism and constructed as a European city, dense, crammed, and intense. The dream-space it offered was employment in a clerical job and the pleasures of strolling along Marine Drive, the crowds and sprawling life in parks and public places, the commuting routines on suburban trains, the tiffin-carriers bringing homemade lunches to the office workers, and the rhythm of life dictated by industrial production.

Today, the desires of modernity in India are different and often go via a job in a call center or an IT company in Delhi and Bangalore, or a job in Singapore or KL—ultimately aspiring to end up in California. The new economy in India and the current notions of modernity are played out in the extensive suburban spaces of Delhi and Bangalore— in polycentric conurbations with shopping malls and bungalows, negotiated by cars and connected by wide roads.

Contemporary Mumbai with its congestion and disintegrating industrial economy does not look like a winner in the race for foreign investment. There is a stark, almost dystopian symbolism in the fact that the while the Parsi community is dying in a genetic implosion brought about through strictly administered rules of in-community marriage, Thackeray's thugs impose both their own law and their unique brand of violent enforcement of ethnic order on large parts of the city, showing little regard for the police or the procedures of the law commanded so deftly by generations of Parsi lawyers.

I realize that this essay in the main seems to feed into the long-standing pessimism in writings on urban India, a pessimism that invariably ends up dreaming back to the order and lost innocence of the colonial city. So let me conclude by emphasizing that I do not think that the iconoclasm and unashamed enjoyment of difference and cultural impurities is dead in Bombay. It is, rather, trying to find a new language in which to express itself and maybe produce a new set of urban utopias.

In 2001, the film *Split Wide Open,* directed by Dev Benegal, created quite a debate and stir in Bombay mainly because it brought out a whole range of taboos in the open—incest, homosexuality, pedophilia. The film is about the creation of a fictitious talk show that seeks to reveal the darkest secrets of the city to its titillated and outraged audience through stories researched and supplied by local brokers and agents— men of the slums and the popular world. People from all walks of life sit on a stage, their faces in darkness, before a live audience and narrate scandalous stories of domestic abuse and transgressive sex. The film is merciless and slightly sensationalist in its exposure of the hypocrisy and the endemic violence that is the foundation of the city's daily life—not the spectacular public violence of the Shiv Sena and others—but the everyday and domestic violence against women, children, and the poor. This iconoclastic film uses the language of the streets and the everyday that increasingly is mixed with English terms into something like "Binglish" to great effect. It demonstrates that the classical Bombay with its dream-spaces—and perhaps also the more boorish Mumbai of the 1990s—indeed has been *Split Wide Open* and is engaged in a process of reinventing itself once again.

NOTES

1. For a good account of the early years of Shiv Sena, see Dipankar Gupta, *Nativism in a Metropolis* (Delhi: Manohar, 1982). For a hagiographical "insider" account see Vaibhav Purandare, *The Sena Story* (Mumbai: Business Publications, 1999).

2. Thomas Blom Hansen *Wages of Violence: Naming and Identity in Postcolonial Bombay* (Princeton, N.J.: Princeton University Press, 2001).

3. Gyan Prakash, "The Idea of Bombay," Department of History, Princeton University, 2002.

4. I have developed this point at some length in "Sovereigns beyond the State: On Legality and Authority in Urban India," in *Sovereign Bodies: Citizens, Migrants, and States in the Postcolonial World,* ed. Thomas Blom Hansen and Finn Stepputat (Princeton, N.J.: Princeton University Press, 2005).

5. Georges Bataille's work on sovereignty was written in the early 1950s but was not published until the 1970s as volume 8 *(La Souverainite)* in *Oeuvres Complètes* (1970–88). The text referred to here is the English translation, republished in 1993.

6. In Lacanian usage the *objet petit a* stands for the irreducible sign of the Real, i.e., the frightening and fascinating dimensions that cannot be symbolized and encompassed within a prevailing social-cultural order, and therefore prevents the closure of identities and cultural horizons.

7. *Times of India,* October 10, 1983.

8. Cover story, "The Dons Also Rise," *The Week,* October 28, 1984.

BIBLIOGRAPHY

Bataille, Georges. 1993. *The Accursed Share.* Vols. 2 and 3. New York: Zone Books. Original in French in *La Souverainite,* vol. 8, in *Oeuvres Complètes* (Paris: Gallimard, 1970–88).

Gupta, Dipankar. *Nativism in a Metropolis.* Delhi: Manohar Publishers, 1982.

Hansen, Thomas, Blom. *Wages of Violence. Naming and Identity in postcolonial Bombay.* Princeton, N.J.: Princeton University Press, 2001.

Hansen, Thomas Blom, and Finn Stepputat, eds. 2005. *Sovereign Bodies: Citizens, Migrants, and States in the Postcolonial World.* Princeton, N.J.: Princeton University Press.

Kojève, Alexander. 1969. *Introduction to the Reading of Hegel.* Assembled by Raymond Queneau. Ed. Allan Bloom. Trans. James H. Nichols Jr. New York: Basic Books.

Mbembe, Achille. 2003. " Necropolitics." *Public Culture* 15, no. 1: 11–40.

Prakash, Gyan. 2002. "The Idea of Bombay." Department of History, Princeton University.

Purandare, Vaibhav. 1999. *The Sena Story.* Mumbai: Business Publications.

Singha, Radhika. 1998. *A Despotism of Law.* Delhi: Oxford University Press.

Žižek, Slavoj. 1993. *Tarrying with the Negative.* Durham, N.C.: Duke University Press.

Rushdie beyond the Veil

Toward the conclusion of Salman Rushdie's prodigious text *Midnight's Children,* Padma, the narrator's audience and interlocutor exclaims, "Oof mister . . . that's too much women!"[1] The phrase captures the tenor of the novel, in which ethics and humor are rendered coterminous, and in which female characters accrue more poignancy than any other midnight's child. The narrator, Saleem Sinai, catalogs the women who have constructed the peculiarities of his history, and who both represent and do not represent the vagaries of the Indian subcontinent:

> How are we to understand my too-many women? As the multiple faces of Bharat-Mata? Or as even more . . . as the dynamic aspect of maya, as cosmic energy . . . ? (*MC,* 467)

A novel that begins with the brilliant trope of the intimacy engendered through a perforated sheet continues its conflation of genre and gender as its language perforates the veil.

The perforating quality of Rushdie's narrative is perhaps best exemplified in the way that the text does not seem to date: even close to twenty-five years after its publication, *Midnight's Children* still has the ability to arrest its readership, making the reader complicit in the dark comedy of historical experience. I find a return to *Midnight's Children* startlingly rejuvenating, whereas wading through the untold miseries of a later text such as Mistry's *A Fine Balance,* for example, leaves me with a surprising and perverse affection for Indira Gandhi. In contrast, Rushdie's study of the consequences and the casualties of partition— both in 1947 and in 1971—are on a par with those of Saadat Hussain Manto and Bapsi Sidhwa. Here, we must note that postcolonial narrative does indeed replicate the anxieties of empire represented by colonial discourse itself, where the innumerable veils of India are represented as a figure for cultural terror. Edward Thompson supplies an uncanny image for this fear:

> Many Englishmen in India must have had my experience. They have been puzzling over the problem, honestly anxious

to find out where the point of exasperation—no, more than exasperation, of severance—came—and to see if anything could be done. Then they have thought that they have found it—yes, it was here, see! They have pushed hard, only to find that they have gone through a curtain painted like a wall, to find a real wall, granite and immovable, behind.[2]

It takes a postcolonial writer like Rushdie to illustrate that the granite is in fact as illusory as the curtain and represents an equally treacherous reality.

When the University of Michigan invited me to participate in a symposium celebrating Salman Rushdie and the Royal Shakespeare Company's performance of *Midnight's Children,* I began my brief comments with an anecdote that indicated a debt of gratitude to Mr. Rushdie. A few years after the publication of *Shame* in 1983 I had submitted an essay for consideration to a learned journal that shall remain unnamed. The journal took its time in doing its reading, and—shortly before the explosive emergence of *The Satanic Verses* in 1988—returned it to me with a polite letter of rejection. Rushdie writes well, I was told, but "she" is really not sufficiently known, and she is not a recognized contemporary writer. I was as thrilled with that conflation of gender as I trust Rushdie will be himself: it is one of the sadnesses of in my life that I failed to save that letter. In any case, I need to thank the author for being the means through which the American academy could present him to me, as it were, in drag.

The very same symposium has made me accrue yet another debt. When the organizers of the event attempted to put together a volume of the proceedings, they urged some of their more tardy participants (such as myself) by sending us transcriptions of our talks. My comments had been scattered, as they frequently are, and I had sought to discuss the figure of the veil as a mode both of empowerment and of disempowerment. In the process, I had used the wry refrain, "I'm a Pakistani, and I am a Muslim." Neither term has to do with nationalism or belief but simply a cultural grounding and a secular reality principle that knows the territories of my memory. The transcriber, however, had more imagination than I. My refrain was astonishingly rephrased. I had been infinitely translated and I can only quote: "Suddenly, life became infinitely simpler for me to be able to say, for better or for worse, I am Bugs Bunny and I am a Muslim." Bugs Bunny! What a wonderful Rushdie-esque transmogrification! And further, a fine illustration that few Pakistanis can aspirate their "p's"! I knew that I would be using the epistemological value of that formulation in many a pedagogical situation to come, so on that front too, I owe an indirect debt of thanks to you, Mr. Rushdie.

The opening veil of *Midnight's Children* is of course the perforated sheet through which the narrator's grandparents, Naseem and Aadam Axiz, first learn piecemeal touch, voice, and, finally, love. The reader is presented this embodiment through Saleem as Scheherazade, so that the deathliness of storytelling is made coterminous with intimacy:

> And there are so many stories to tell, too many, such an excess of intertwined lives events miracles places rumours, so dense a commingling of the improbable and the mundane. . . . Consumed multitudes are jostling and shoving inside me; and guided only by the memory of a large white bed sheet with a roughly circular hole some seven inches in diameter cut into the center, clutching at the dream of that holey, mutilated square of linen, which is my talisman, my open-sesame, I must commence at the business of re-making my life from the point at which it really began, some thirty-two years before anything as obvious as *present,* as my clock-ridden, crime-stained birth. (*MC,* 4)

The peculiarity of the text is precisely the manner in which characters are inevitably casualties of their own stories but the tales themselves survive, and not only through the medium of Saleem's narration. In fact, a principle of multiplicity is curiously at home with an urge to negation, so that it is no surprise at all that most human relations end in acute if not tragic disappointment. Nor can such failures be solely credited as the responsibility of postindependence history, which sits on the cusp of being either dangerously too new or dangerously too nostalgic for precolonial times.

Midnight's Children is in its energies fated to repetition: the partition of 1947 that engenders independent India and Pakistan is replicated in the brutal war of 1971 that results in Bangladesh. These historical perforations are carefully matched in the narrative by choreographed human encounters that attempt contact, approach union, and then dissipate. The opening encounter between Aadam and Nasim Aziz is if anything only more traumatically reproduced in the exchange between narrator Saleem and his titular sister, the Brass Monkey. That Saleem is a changeling and actually the son of the colonialist Methwold is evident early on in the text to an attentive reader, although the novel itself achingly delays a literal revelation of the gothic facts. It thus allows its idiom to intensify an incest that is not incest, just as the Brass Monkey becomes more peculiarly erotic when she is transmuted into Jamila Singer by Pakistan, the Land of the Pure. She becomes the beloved singing voice of Pakistan, and once again, identity is quickened and shaped by the entry of a perforated sheet.

While Saleem is constantly accompanied by women, from Padma to Parvati the witch, it is his relation with his sister that remains the most veiled and overdetermined in the novel. When she sings in public, she is shielded by a "famous, all-concealing, white silk chadar, the curtain or veil, heavily embroidered in gold brocade work and religious calligraphy. . . . at its very center, [they] had cut a hole. Diameter: three inches. Circumference: embroidered in finest gold thread. That was how the history of our family once again became the fate of a nation, because when Jamila sang with her lips pressed against the brocaded aperture, Pakistan fell in love with a fifteen-year-old girl whom it only ever glimpsed through a gold-and-white perforated sheet" (*MC,* 358–59). Saleem is of course the voyeur of such a history, because he occupies the strange position of being at both sides of the sheet at the same time.

He can never, however, work his way through the perforation into a "happily ever after" conclusiveness: despite his attempts to unravel the mythmaking of their siblinghood, "there were other truths which had become more important because they had been sanctified by time; and although there was no need for shame or horror, he saw both emotions on her forehead, he smelt them on her skin, and what was worse, he could feel and smell in an on himself" (*MC,* 372). Saleem frequently addresses himself in the third person—an alienation effect in the narrative—and at this point one that underscores the empowerment of Jamila's veil, which declares that there is no difference at all between a figurative and a literal incest. A family tree, in other words, need not be biological: intimacy is all.

Saleem has to translate this lesson painfully, step by step, into his rereading of history after the traumas of Bangladesh and his experience in the Sundarbans. The Brass Monkey / Jamila Singer is to disappear behind a final veil, a convent, and Saleem must confront how even his erotic engagement may have been allegorical: "But there are cracks and gaps . . . had I, by then, begun to see that my love for Jamila Singer had been, in a sense, a mistake? Had I already understood how I had simply transferred on to her shoulders the adoration which I now perceived to be a vaulting, all-encompassing love of country? When was it that I realized that my truly-incestuous feelings were for my true birth-sister, India herself . . . ?" (*MC,* 444). It is interesting to note that Mother India of venerability has been modified by modernity into Sister India, suggesting that a degree of sibling rivalry can now obtain between the stories of the nation and those of the individual.

As a consequence, the powerful veiling and concomitant loss of Jamila Singer leads in a circuitous route to the unveiling of India, despite the intrusion of the Widow India and her Emergency. One is compelled to recall not only Rushdie's own vertiginous articulation of unveiling in his essays collected under the title *Imaginary Homelands,* but their congruence with the crucial questions raised quietly by Benedict Anderson in his still seminal work on nationalism, *Imagined Communities.* Much as *Midnight's Children* raises the embarrassment of the casualties of love in its narrative, Anderson poses the naked question: "In an age when it is common for progressive, cosmopolitan intellectuals . . . to insist on the near-pathological character of nationalism, its roots in fear and hatred of the Other, and its affinities with racism, it is useful to remind ourselves that nations inspire love, and often profoundly self-sacrificing love. The cultural products of nationalism . . . show this love very clearly in thousands of different forms and styles. On the other hand, how truly rare it is to find analogous nationalist products expressing fear and loathing."[3] Saleem learns through a complex process of chutnification—a veiling of its own—to place the impetus toward "fear and loathing" beyond apocalypse and into a gesture toward compassion, or uneasy irresolution.

Similarly, in Rushdie's darkest novel, *Shame,* the narrative seems forced into an unresolved and dialogic relation with its own subject. The subject questions the novel's authority; the language the two share is equally threadbare. Neither can move beyond the veil of the other, although both appear painfully nude. Instead, narrative and subject functions turn to the idiom of a court of appeal in the vain hope that their chronologies may continue: "*Outsider! Trespasser! You have no right to this subject! . . . I know: nobody ever arrested me. Nor are they ever likely to. Poacher! Pirate! We reject your authority. We know you, with your foreign language wrapped around you like a flag, what can you tell us but lies?* I reply with more questions: is history to be considered the property of the participants solely? In what courts are such claims staked, what boundary commissions map out the territories?"[4] The voices in question here are as perforating as those in *Midnight's Children:* even though *Shame's* narrative is deliberately more loveless and more monolithic, it nevertheless plays as vitally with what can and cannot be hidden, what is and what is not available to historical forgetfulness. The postcolonial nation Pakistan, rendered archly allegorical as "Pekkavistan," is allowed none of the imaginative generosity Rushdie bestowed upon his representations of India, but the territory itself can still teeter to take Rushdie and his story beyond the veil.

The actual retelling of the Zulfikar Ali Bhutto and General Zia ul-Haq encounter, translated into the story of Iskander Harrappa and General Raza Hyde, bears scant interest today. *Shame*'s plot is indeed embarrassingly dated: much as *Midnight's Children* enriches with each decade, *Shame* atrophies in its own journalistic allegoricalisism. Its narrative, however, can redeem itself through a conscious recognition of its own apertures, of an acknowledgment of dischronology. Not surprisingly, this disjuncture occurs most frequently through the formal recognition of women: "I had thought, before I began, that what I had on my hands was an almost excessively masculine tale, a saga of sexual rivalry, ambition, power, patronage, betrayal, death, revenge. But the women seem to have taken over; they marched in from the peripheries of the story to demand an inclusion of their own tragedies, histories and comedies, obliging me to couch my narrative in all manner of sinuous complexities, to see my 'male' plot refracted, so to speak, through the prisms of its reverse and 'female' side" (*Shame,* 173). The aura of disingenuousness of such a claim is always dissipated by the dynamic of gender in the text, which, despite the sad apocalypse in which it concludes, seems complicit in Rushdie's desire to seek for the narrative aperture, to locate the opening.

Had I world enough and time, I would take on the extraordinary openings, the veilings and unveilings, that constitute the moving and very loving text of 1988, *The Satanic Verses*. Since I do not, I will focus instead on the Ayesha episode in the novel, which moves away from the miracle of Muhammad into a contemporary subcontinental translation of miracle. The curiosity of the narrative is the manner in which it can shield and unshield the prophet at the same time, giving devotion while opening language to a postmodern tenderness. And the prophet is represented in close to sufistic terms: "The businessman: looks like he should, high forehead, eagle nose, broad in the shoulders, narrow in the hip. Average height, brooding, dressed in two pieces of plain cloth, each four ells in length, one draped about his body, the other over his shoulder. Large eyes; long lashes like a girl's. His strides can seem too long for his legs, but he's a light-footed man."[5] In the Verses, this Prophet is radically veiled and occupies the cross-gendered and cross-generic terrain that can declare: God is absolutely one.

For a storyteller, of course, that is a most astounding notion. It supplies an alternative narrative that should not have currency, because of the possible efficiency of its grammar. Certainly in *The Satanic Verses* the grandee of pre-Islamic Mecca dreads Islam because of its capacity to represent the one: "He remembers the big one, the slave, Bilal: how his master asked him . . . to enumerate the gods. 'One,' he answered, in that huge musical voice. Blasphemy, punishable by death. They stretched him out in the fairground with a boulder on his chest. How many did you say? One, he repeated, one. . . . Why do I fear Mahound? For that: one one one, his terrifying singularity. Whereas I am always divided, always two or three or fifteen" (*SV*, 102). When Bilal the slave musically asserts a unitary epistemology, he not only endorses his prophet's narrative but further witnesses the latter's ability to strip into secrecy.

It is such secrecy that the poignancy of the Ayesha episode in *The Satanic Verses* supplies the reader. Her veil is perhaps one of the most touching of all, for she is clad in butterflies, and takes charge of the most doomed and evanescent of apocalyptic stories. This tale is based on an extraordinary historical event that took place in Karachi, Pakistan: The Hawkes Bay case occurred in February 1983, when thirty-eight Shia Muslims walked into the Arabian Sea, devotedly expecting that the waters would part, letting the pilgrims walk to the holy city of Basra and then to the sacred site of Karbala itself. Their inspiration was Naseem Fatima, a young woman who declared herself to be in visionary contact with the Twelfth Imam of the Shias. The Karachi police force arrived at Hawkes Bay to find that most of the pilgrims had drowned: in the curious surrealism that can accompany postcolonial history, they decided to arrest the survivors because the latter had tried to leave the nation without legal papers. This episode however, was not yet done. Akbar S. Ahmed records that "rich Shias, equally impressed [by the surviving pilgrims] presented them with gifts, including rare copies of the Holy Quran. Naseem's promise that they would visit Karbala without worldly means was fulfilled."[6] The girl prophet of *The Satanic Verses,* Ayesha, echoes the name of the prophet Muhammad's daughter, and lives in a village called Titlipur, "village of butterflies." It is here that the angel Gabriel instructs her to undertake the miraculous journey to Mecca, but will only speak to her in the language of popular film songs. "Everything will be desired of us," Ayesha enjoins the villagers, "and everything will be given to us also" (*SV*, 225). Of course there are skeptics, both in the village and in the subcontinent, for whom the Ayesha hajj is a transgression of not just religious but national stability as well, so that Ayesha joins the ranks of midnight's children. One skeptic is the village landlord, who wishes to explode the myth of miracle by buying Ayesha an air ticket to Mecca. His argument is that of mockery: "Partition was quite a disaster here on land. Quite a few guys died, you might remember. You think it will be different in the water?" (*SV,* 501). The text is postmodern enough to leave the question of miracle completely open-ended; it is hardly important to the reader that some of the more skeptical survivors provide a testimonial for the parting of the waters: "Just when my strength failed and I thought I would surely die there in the water, I saw it with my own eyes; I saw the sea divide, like hair being combed; and they were all there, far away, walking away from me" (*SV,* 504). The feminized gesture of "hair being combed" takes the discourse of miracle away from the grandiloquence back to a local habitation and name.

Much as in *Midnight's Children* antiapocalypse, Saleem Sinai moves beyond his own veils and those of his history. So the Ayesha episode in *The Satanic Verses* suggests an alternative reading to the trope of opening. The overdetermined "parting" with which the chapter is named—parting, separation, partition, miracle, opening—culminates in a death scene that rereads each term. The skeptic landlord, Ayesha's tempter and old antagonist, is literally on his deathbed. He then undergoes a figurative drowning that transmutes his understanding of the language of miracle and the ecstasy that may attend it:

> Then the sea poured over him, and he was in the water beside Ayesha. . . . "Open," she was crying. . . ."Open," she said. He closed.
>
> He was a fortress with clanging gates.—He was drowning.—She was drowning too. He saw the water fill her mouth, heard it begin to gurgle into her lungs. Then something within him refused that, made a different choice, and at the instant his heart broke, he opened.
>
> His body split apart from his Adam's apple to his groin, so that she could reach deep within him, and now she was open, they all were, and at the moment of their opening the waters parted, and they walked to Mecca across the bed of the Arabian Sea. (*SV,* 506–7)

For the reader who has endured the claustrophobia—albeit wryly comic—of the Jahiliya and the London chapters, this opening registers as a pool of respite, not even as an enactment of magic realism, but rather as a wistful tribute toward it.

And perhaps that is finally Rushdie's real engagement with the contemporary novel, the ability to assume the magical and then allow that language to dissipate around the narrative as it unfolds. Rushdie as Salome is not quite such a facetious idea as it may first appear. Whose head is in the offing, no one knows; it frequently is his protagonists', and at one point, it was his own. But the veils keep drawing in many vertiginous directions, so that the crossings of gender and culture make locations of equilibrium the greatest of available miracles. Is it "too much women" or too much of that embarrassing term, humanity, in a text like *Midnight's Children*? Is modernity and its several attendant "posts" (postmodernism, postcolonialism, etc.) one of the veils that Rushdie has crossed? (One hopes, of course, not into the self-parodic mode that *The Ground beneath Her Feet* threateningly suggests.) In fact, I think of the performance of *Midnight's Children* with a twinge of regret—for readers who have loved and taught the text, there was a stridency, a documentation to the spectacle that lost the nuances of the novel's language. Strangely enough, the written voice was far more alive, rich, and comic than when it was a spoken.

Let me conclude with an exemplary unveiling at the exhausted end of *Midnight's Children* when in an idiom of great aesthetic dignity Saleem Sinai declares, "Yes, they will trample me underfoot, the numbers marching one two three, four hundred million five hundred six, reducing me to specks to voiceless dust, just as, in all good time, they will trample my son who is not my son, and his son who will not be his, and his who will not be his, until the thousand and first generation, until a thousand and one midnights have bestowed their terrible gifts and a thousand and one children have died, because it is the privilege and the curse of midnight's children to be both masters and victims of their times" (*MC*, 533). This conclusion, with its enriching category of negatives—a genealogy predicated on "not"—resonates with a colonial echo. It is a passage to India. Fielding and Aziz, at the conclusion of that astonishing narrative, ask with remarkable naïveté, "Why can't we be friends now?" The answer they receive is categorical: "But the horses didn't want it—they swerved apart; the earth didn't want it, sending up rocks through which the riders must pass single file; the temples, the tank, the jail . . . they didn't want it, they said in their hundred voices, 'no, not yet,' and the sky said, 'no, not there.'"[7]

When I wish to locate Rushdie beyond the veil, I trust it is interpreted in no simplistic ideology of humanism, a term too much abused, nor in sophistries of language, too much discussed, too much explained. Instead, I draw your attention to my continuing affection for *Midnight's Children* and to how its chutnification of languages and cultures can still construct precarious structures of human contact. I still read, I still teach. I am Bugs Bunny, after all.

NOTES

1. *Midnight's Children* (London: Jonathan Cape, 1980), 467.

2. Edward Thompson, *The Other Side of the Medal* (New York: Harcourt, Brace, 1926, rpt. Westport, Conn.: Greenwood, 1974), 26–27.

3. Benedict Anderson, *Imagined Communities: Reflections on the Origin and Spread of Nationalism* (London: Verso, 1983), 129.

4. Salman Rushdie, *Shame* (London: Picador, 1983), 28.

5. Salman Rushdie, *The Satanic Verses* (London: Viking, 1988), 93.

6. Akbar S. Ahmad, *Pakistan Society: Islam, Ethnicity, and Leadership in South Asia* (Karachi: Oxford University Press 1986), 56.

7. E. M. Forster, *A Passage to India* (London: Harcourt, Brace and World, 1924), 322.

SHASHI THAROOR

Rushdie's "Overartist"

Indianness from Midnight to the Millennium

Nearly twenty Valentine's Days ago, Iran's Ayatollah Khomeini pronounced a fatwa, an Islamic edict, calling for the death of Salman
Rushdie—and made the Indian-born British author of *The Satanic
Verses* the most famous writer in the world. Yet the extent to which
this controversy has dominated our perception of his work is itself an
injustice. Mention Rushdie, and some see a stirring symbol of the cause
of freedom of expression in the face of intolerant dogma; others, particularly in the Islamic world, find a blasphemous crusader for secular-
ist social subversion. Neither image may be inaccurate, but reducing
him to this emblematic figure has only obscured his true literary contribution—as, quite simply, one of the best and most important novelists of our time. As an Indian novelist, I can only repeat what Waugh
said of Wodehouse: he is the head of my profession.

For Salman Rushdie has brought an astonishing new voice into the
world of English-language fiction, a voice whose language and concerns stretched the boundaries of the possible in English literature. His
heritage is derived from the polyglot tumult of multiethnic, postcolonial India; his intellectual convictions owe as much to Nehruvian nationalism and the eclecticism of the Sufi mystics as to any source West
of the Suez; his style combines a formal English education with the ca-
dences of the Indian oral storytelling tradition, the riches of Latin
American magic realism, and the extravagant fabulism of the *Arabian
Nights*. Both in his life and in his writing, Rushdie has stood for intermingling and interchange, displacement and transfiguration, migration
and renewal. He recalled and reinvented his roots while thriving in his
own uprootedness. With *Midnight's Children* he brought a larger
world—a teeming, myth-infused, gaudy, exuberant, many-hued, and
restless world—past the immigration inspectors of English literature.
And he has enriched this new homeland with breathtaking, risk-rid-
den, imaginative prose of rare brilliance and originality.

In eight novels (of which I have only skipped the first, the reput-
edly impenetrable *Grimus*) Rushdie has developed his characteristic
concerns with the great issues of our time. Themes of migration, inno-

vation, conversion, separation, and transformation suffuse his work: exploration and discovery, faith and doubt, pluralism and purity, yearning and desire infuse his fiction. And with all of Rushdie's novels, his story is also about the telling of stories. Above all, it would seem, of Indian stories, for Indian history, society, and contemporary politics are a rich lode he has profitably mined in all his books. India is, as ever, the intersection of the many strands of Rushdie's intellectual heritage, the womb of his imagination.

India—"that country without a middle register, that continuum entirely composed of extremes"—is itself a character in many of his books. The author's farewell to it in *The Ground beneath Her Feet* is unbearably poignant: "India, my *terra infirma*. . . . India, my too-muchness, my everything at once, my mother, my father and my first great truth. . . . India, fount of my imagination, source of my savagery, breaker of my heart. Goodbye." But with Rushdie India always leads to the world; it is a mini-universe for a writer whose concerns are universal. "[T]o provide for the planet's soul, there is India. One goes there as one goes to the bank, to refill the pocketbook of the psyche."

But what does the novelist fill it with? In a sadly overlooked passage of *The Satanic Verses*, Salman Rushdie writes of "the eclectic, hybridized nature of the Indian artistic tradition." Under the Mughals, he says, artists of different faiths and traditions were brought from many parts of India to work on a painting. One hand would paint the mosaic floors, another the human figures, a third the cloudy skies: "individual identity was submerged to create a many-headed, many-brushed Overartist who, literally, *was* Indian painting." This evocative image could as well be applied to the nature of Indianness itself, the product of the same hybrid culture. How, after all, can one summarize the idea of the Indian identity? Any truism about India can be immediately contradicted by another truism about India. The country's national motto, emblazoned on its governmental crest, is "Satyameva Jayaté": Truth Alone Triumphs. The question remains, however: whose truth? It is a question to which there are at least a billion answers—if the last census hasn't undercounted us again.

I raise the question of truth because, in the 2004 political campaigns in northern India, then Prime Minister Vajpayee apparently described the Congress Party leader, Sonia Gandhi, as a foreigner. When protests erupted, the PM said he was not casting aspersions on the leader of the opposition, merely stating a fact. But is it a fact? The renewed debate on the issue of Sonia Gandhi's eligibility to lead the country has brought to the forefront a vital question that has, in different ways, often engaged me—the question, "Who is an Indian?"

The last time this issue grabbed the headlines was in 2000, when a crisis erupted in the Congress Party over the claim by three powerful Congress politicians, Sharad Pawar, Purno Sangma, and Tariq Anwar—with classic Congress secularism, a Hindu, a Christian, and a Muslim—that Mrs. Gandhi was unfit to be Prime Minister because she was born in Italy. In the extraordinary letter they delivered to her and leaked to the newspapers, the three party leaders declared, "It is not possible that a country of 980 million, with a wealth of education, competence and ability, can have anyone other than an Indian, born of Indian soil, to head its government." They went so far as to ask her to propose a constitutional amendment requiring that the offices of president and Prime Minister be held only by natural-born Indian citizens.

Of course there has been no such amendment, and the three Congress leaders are now ex-Congress leaders, having founded the Nationalist Congress Party instead to add to the splendid alphabet soup of political parties in our country. But their territorial notion of Indian nationhood is a curious one on many counts, and particularly so coming from long-standing members of the Indian National Congress, a party that was founded under a Scottish-born president, Allan Octavian Hume, in 1885 and among whose most redoubtable leaders (and elected presidents) was Annie Besant, who was born English, and Maulana Abul Kalam Azad, who was born in Mecca. Even more curious is the implicit repudiation of the views of the Congress's greatest-ever leader, Mahatma Gandhi, who tried to make the party a representative microcosm of an India he saw as eclectic, agglomerative, and diverse.

The three musketeers of the nativist revolt did, of course, anticipate this latter criticism. So they went out of their way to reinvent the Mahatma on their side. "India has always lived in the spirit of the Mahatma's words, 'Let the winds from all over sweep into my room,'" they wrote with fealty if not accuracy. "But again he said, 'I will not be swept off my feet.' We accept with interest and humility the best which we can gather from the north, south, east or west and we absorb them into our soil. But our inspiration, our soul, our honour, our pride, our dignity, is rooted in our soil. It has to be of this earth." The contradiction between their paraphrase of the Mahatma's views (absorbing the best from all directions) and their emotive "rooting" of "honour, pride and dignity" in the "soil" of "this earth" is so blatant it hardly needs pointing out. Yet it suffers a further inaccuracy: by law, even a "natural-born Indian" is one who has just one grandparent born in undivided India, as defined by the Government of India Act, 1935. You do not have to be of "this soil" to be an Indian by birth.

But Sonia Gandhi is, of course, an Indian by marriage and natural-ization, not birth. So the usual chauvinists and xenophobes—not to mention the political opportunists of other stripes—have been quick to jump on the bandwagon started by the soil-sprung triumvirate. But is her Westernness immutably irreconcilable with their Indianness? In *The Ground beneath Her Feet* Rushdie brilliantly translates "disorienta-tion" as "loss of the East." "Ask any navigator: the east is what you sail by. Lose the east and you lose your bearings, your certainties, your knowledge of what is and what may be, perhaps even your life." But not for Rushdie the flawed simplicity of the conventional encounters between East and West. The West, he points out, "was in Bombay from the beginning," in a land "where West, East, North and South had always been scrambled like codes, like eggs, and so Westernness was a legitimate part of Ormus, a Bombay part, inseparable from the rest of him."

So the truth may lie in a simple insight: as I have written in my book *India: From Midnight to the Millennium,* the singular thing about India is that you can only speak of it in the plural. There are, in the hackneyed phrase, many Indias. Everything exists in countless variants. If Americans can cite the national motto "E Pluribus Unum," Indians can suggest "E Pluribus Pluribum." There is no single standard, no fixed stereotype, no "one way." This pluralism is acknowledged in the way India arranges its own affairs: all groups, faiths, tastes, and ideolo-gies survive and contend for their place in the sun. At a time when most developing countries opted for authoritarian models of govern-ment to promote nation-building and to direct development, India chose to be a multiparty democracy. And despite many stresses and strains, including twenty-two months of autocratic rule during a "state of Emergency" declared by Prime Minister Indira Gandhi in 1975, a multiparty democracy—freewheeling, rumbustious, corrupt, and inefficient, perhaps, but nonetheless flourishing—India has remained.

One result is that India strikes many as maddening, chaotic, inefficient, and seemingly unpurposeful as it muddles through the opening years of the twenty-first century. Another, though, is that In-dia is not just a country, it is an adventure, one in which all avenues are open and everything is possible. "India," wrote the British historian E. P. Thompson, "is perhaps the most important country for the future of the world. All the convergent influences of the world run through this society. . . . There is not a thought that is being thought in the West or East that is not active in some Indian mind."

That Indian mind has been shaped by remarkably diverse forces: ancient Hindu tradition, myth, and scripture; the impact of Islam and

Christianity; and two centuries of British colonial rule. The result is unique. Many observers have been astonished by India's survival as a pluralist state. But India could hardly have survived as anything else. Pluralism is a reality that emerges from the very nature of the country; it is a choice made inevitable by India's geography and reaffirmed by its history.

One of the few generalizations that can safely be made about India is that nothing can be taken for granted about the country. Not even its name: for the word *India* comes from the river Indus, which flows in Pakistan. That anomaly is easily explained, for what is today Pakistan was part of India until the country was partitioned by the departing British in 1947. (Yet each explanation breeds another anomaly. Pakistan was created as a homeland for India's Muslims, but at least till very recently, there were more Muslims in India than in Pakistan.)

With diversity emerging from its geography and inscribed in its history, India was made for pluralist democracy. It is not surprising, then, that the political life of modern India has been rather like traditional Indian music: the broad basic rules are firmly set, but within them one is free to improvise, unshackled by a written score. The music of India is the collective anthem of a hybrid civilization.

Over fifty-four years ago, at midnight on August 15, 1947, as the flames of communal hatred blazed across the land, independent India was born as its first Prime Minister, Jawaharlal Nehru, proclaimed "a tryst with destiny—a moment which comes but rarely in history, when we pass from the old to the new, when an age ends and when the soul of a nation, long suppressed, finds utterance." With those words he launched India on a remarkable experiment in governance—remarkable because it was happening at all. "India," Winston Churchill once barked, "is merely a geographical expression. It is no more a single country than the Equator." Churchill was rarely right about India, but it is true that no other country in the world embraces the extraordinary mixture of ethnic groups, the profusion of mutually incomprehensible languages, the varieties of topography and climate, the diversity of religions and cultural practices, and the range of levels of economic development that India does.

And yet India is more than the sum of its contradictions. It is a country held together, in Nehru's words, "by strong but invisible threads. . . . She is a myth and an idea," he wrote—Nehru always feminized India—"a dream and a vision, and yet very real and present and pervasive."

It has been over sixty years since that midnight moment when the British Empire in India came to an end amid the traumatic carnage of partition with Pakistan and the sectarian violence that accompanied it. Yet, in these last five decades of independence, many thoughtful observers have seen a country more conscious than ever of what divides it: religion, region, caste, language, ethnicity. What makes India, then, a nation?

Let me turn again to an Italian example. No, not *that* Italian example. Amid the popular ferment that made an Italian nation out of a mosaic of principalities and statelets, one Italian nationalist memorably wrote, "We have created Italy. Now all we need to do is to create Italians." Oddly enough, no Indian nationalist succumbed to the temptation to express the same thought—"We have created India; now all we need to do is to create Indians."

Such a sentiment would not, in any case, have occurred to Nehru, that preeminent voice of Indian nationalism, because he believed that India and Indians had existed for millennia before he gave words to their longings; he would never have spoken of "creating" India or Indians, merely of being the agent for the reassertion of what had always existed but had been long suppressed. Nonetheless, the India that was born in 1947 was in a very real sense a new creation: a state that had made fellow citizens of the Ladakhi and the Laccadivian for the first time, that divided Punjabi from Punjabi for the first time, that asked the Keralite peasant to feel allegiance to a Kashmiri Pandit ruling in Delhi, also for the first time. Nehru would not have written of the challenge of "creating" Indians, but creating Indians was what, in fact, the nationalist movement did.

When India celebrated the forty-ninth anniversary of its independence from British rule in 1996, its then Prime Minister, H. D. Deve Gowda, stood at the ramparts of Delhi's sixteenth-century Red Fort and delivered the traditional Independence Day address to the nation in Hindi, India's "national language." Eight other Prime Ministers had done exactly the same thing forty-eight times before him, but what was unusual this time was that Deve Gowda, a southerner from the state of Karnataka, spoke to the country in a language of which he did not know a word. Tradition and politics required a speech in Hindi, so he gave one—the words having been written out for him in his native Kannada script, in which they, of course, made no sense.

Such an episode is almost inconceivable elsewhere, but it represents the best of the oddities that help make India India. Only in India could a country be ruled by a man who does not understand its "national language"; only in India, for that matter, is there a "national language" that half the population does not understand; and only in India could this particular solution be found to enable the Prime Minister to address his people. One of Indian cinema's finest "playback singers," the Keralite K. J. Yesudas, sang his way to the top of the Hindi music charts with lyrics in that language written in the Malayalam script for him, but to see the same practice elevated to the Prime Ministerial address on Independence Day was a startling affirmation of Indian pluralism.

We are all minorities in India. A typical Indian stepping off a train, a Hindi-speaking Hindu male from the Gangetic plain state of Uttar Pradesh, might cherish the illusion that he represents the "majority community," to use an expression much favored by the less industrious of our journalists. But he does not. As a Hindu he belongs to the faith adhered to by some 82 percent of the population, but a majority of the country does not speak Hindi; a majority does not hail from Uttar Pradesh; and if he were visiting, say, Kerala, he would discover that a majority is not even male. Worse, our archetypal UP Hindu has only to mingle with the polyglot, polychrome crowds thronging any of India's major railway stations to realize how much of a minority he really is. Even his Hinduism is no guarantee of majorityhood, because his caste automatically places him in a minority as well: if he is a Brahmin, 90 percent of his fellow Indians are not; if he is a Yadav, 85 percent of Indians are not, and so on.

Or take language. The Constitution of India recognizes twenty-three today (one can see fourteen scripts on the rupee notes), but in fact, there are thirty-five Indian languages that are spoken by more than a million people—and these are *languages,* with their own scripts, grammatical structures, and cultural assumptions, not just dialects (and if were to count dialects within these languages, there are more than twenty-two thousand). Each of the native speakers of these languages is in a linguistic minority, for none enjoys majority status in India. Thanks in part to the popularity of Bombay's Hindi cinema, Hindi is understood, if not always well spoken, by nearly half the population of India, but it is in no sense the language of the majority; indeed, its locutions, gender rules, and script are unfamiliar to most Indians in the south or northeast.

Ethnicity further complicates the notion of a majority community. Most of the time, an Indian's name immediately reveals where he is from and what his mother tongue is; when we introduce ourselves, we are advertising our origins. Despite some intermarriage at the elite levels in the cities, Indians still largely remain endogamous, and a Bengali is easily distinguished from a Punjabi. The difference this reflects is often more apparent than the elements of commonality. A Karnataka Brahmin shares his Hindu faith with a Bihari Kurmi, but feels little identity with him in respect of appearance, dress, customs, tastes, language, or political objectives. At the same time a Tamil Hindu would feel that he has far more in common with a Tamil Christian or Tamil Muslim than with, say, a Haryanvi Jat with whom he formally shares a religion.

Why do I harp on these differences? Only to make the point that Indian nationalism is a rare animal indeed. It is not based on language (since we have at least twenty-three or thirty-five, depending on whether you follow the constitution or the ethnolinguists). It is not based on geography (the "natural" geographical frontiers of India have been hacked by the partition of 1947). It is not based on ethnicity (the "Indian" accommodates a diversity of racial types in which many Indians have more in common with foreigners than with other Indians— Indian Punjabis and Bengalis, for instance, have more in common with Pakistanis and Bangladeshis, respectively, than they do with Poonawalas or Bangaloreans). And it is not based on religion (we are home to every faith known to mankind, and Hinduism—a faith without a national organization, with no established church or ecclesiastical hierarchy, no uniform beliefs or modes of worship—exemplifies as much our diversity as it does our common cultural heritage). Indian nationalism is the nationalism of an idea, the idea of an ever-ever land— emerging from an ancient civilization, united by a shared history, sustained by pluralist democracy.

This land imposes no narrow conformities on its citizens: you can be many things *and* one thing. You can be a good Muslim, a good Keralite, and a good Indian all at once. Our founding fathers wrote a constitution for a dream; we have given passports to our ideals. Where Freudians note the distinctions that arise out of "the narcissism of minor differences," in India we celebrate the commonality of major differences. To stand Michael Ignatieff's famous phrase on its head, we are a land of belonging rather than of blood.

So the idea of India, to use Amartya Sen's phrase, is of one land embracing many. It is the idea that a nation may endure differences of caste, creed, color, culture, cuisine, conviction, costume, and custom, and still rally around a democratic consensus. That consensus is around the simple principle that in a democracy you don't really need to agree—except on the ground rules of how you will disagree. The reason India has survived all the stresses and strains that have beset it for fifty years, and that led so many to predict its imminent disintegration, is that it maintained consensus on how to manage without consensus.

Of course, not all agree with this vision of India. There are those who wish it to become a Hindu Rashtra, a land of and for the Hindu majority; they have made gains in recent elections and in the politics of the street. Secularism is established in India's constitution, but they ask why India should not, like many other Third World countries, find refuge in the assertion of its own religious identity. News stories have chronicled the rise in Indian politics of an intolerant and destructive "Hindutva" movement that assaults India's minorities, especially its Muslims, that destroyed a well-known mosque and conducted horrific attacks on Muslims in the state of Gujarat, where in the twenty-first century men have been slaughtered because of the mark on a forehead or the absence of a foreskin. The votaries of this movement argue that only Hindus can be true Indians; Muslims and Christians, in particular, are deemed insufficiently Indian because their *punyabhoomi,* their holy land, lies outside the soil of India.

It is curious and sad to see the "two-nation theory" advocated by the supporters of partition in the 1940s coming back to life in secular India six decades later. My generation (and Rushdie's) grew up in an India where our sense of nationhood lay in the slogan "unity in diversity." We were brought up to take pluralism for granted, and to reject the communalism that had partitioned the nation when the British left. In rejecting the case for partition, Indian nationalism also rejected the very idea that religion should be a determinant of nationhood. We never fell into the insidious trap of agreeing that, since partition had established a state for Muslims, what remained was a state for Hindus. To accept the idea of India you had to spurn the logic that had divided the country.

Western dictionaries define *secularism* as the absence of religion, but Indian secularism means a profusion of religions, none of which is privileged by the state. Secularism in India does not mean irreligiousness, which even avowedly atheist parties like the Communists or the DMK (Dravida Munnetra Kazhagam) have found unpopular among their voters; indeed, in Calcutta's annual Durga Puja, the youth wings of the Communist parties compete with each other to put up the most lavish Puja *pandals* or pavilions to the Goddess Durga. Rather, it means, in the Indian tradition, multireligiousness. In the Calcutta neighborhood where I lived during my high school years, the wail of the muezzin calling the Islamic faithful to prayer blended with the tinkling bells and chanted mantras at the Hindu Shiva temple nearby and the crackling loudspeakers outside the Sikh *guruduwara* reciting verses from the Granth Sahib. (And St. Paul's Cathedral was only minutes away.)

The irony is that India's secular coexistence was paradoxically made possible by the fact that the overwhelming majority of Indians are Hindus. It is odd to read today of "Hindu fundamentalism," because Hinduism is a religion without fundamentals: no organized church, no compulsory beliefs or rites of worship, no single sacred book. The name itself denotes something less, and more, than a set of theological beliefs. In many languages—French and Persian among them—the word for "Indian" is *Hindu*. Originally *Hindu* simply meant the people beyond the river Sindhu, or Indus. But the Indus is now in Islamic Pakistan; and to make matters worse, the word *Hindu* did not exist in any Indian language till its use by foreigners gave Indians a term for self-definition.

Hinduism is thus the name others applied to the indigenous religion of India (Sanatan Dharma). It embraces an eclectic range of doctrines and practices, from pantheism to agnosticism and from faith in reincarnation to belief in the caste system. But none of these constitutes an obligatory credo for a Hindu: there are none. We have no compulsory dogmas. Hinduism is a civilization, not a creed that can be reduced to commandments.

The sectarian misuse of Hinduism for minority-bashing is especially sad since Hinduism provides the basis for a shared sense of common culture within India that has little to do with religion. The inauguration of a public project, the laying of a foundation stone, or the launching of a ship usually starts with the ritual smashing of a coconut, an auspicious practice in Hinduism but one that most Indians of other faiths cheerfully accept in much the same spirit as a teetotaler acknowledges the role of champagne in a Western celebration. Hindu festivals, from Holi (when friends and strangers of all faiths are sprayed with colored water in a Dionysian ritual) to Deepavali (the festival of lights, firecrackers, and social gambling), have already gone beyond their religious origins to unite Indians of all faiths as a shared experience.

Festivals, *melas, lilas,* all "Hindu" in origin, have become occasions for the mingling of ordinary Indians of all backgrounds; indeed, for generations now, Muslim artisans in the Hindu holy city of Varanasi have made the traditional masks for the annual Ram Lila (the dance-drama depicting the tale of the divine god-king, Rama). Hindu myths like the Ramayana and the Mahabharata provide a common idiom to all Indians, and it was not surprising that when national television broadcast a fifty-two-episode serialization of the Mahabharata, the script was written by a Muslim, Dr. Rahi Masoom Raza. Both Hindus and Muslims throng the tombs and *dargahs* of Sufi Muslim saints. Hindu devotional songs are magnificently sung by the Muslim Dagar brothers; the Hindu Shankar Shambhu invokes Muslim *pirs* as he chants the *qawwali*. Hinduism and Islam are intertwined in Indian life. In the Indian context today, it is possible to say that there is no Hinduism without Islam: the saffron and the green both belong on the Indian flag.

A lovely story that illustrates the cultural synthesis of Hinduism and Islam in India was recounted by two American scholars, Lloyd and Susan Rudolph. It seems an Indian Muslim girl was asked to participate in a small community drama about the life of Lord Krishna, the Hindu god adored by shepherdesses, who dance for his pleasure (and who exemplify through their passion the quest of the devout soul for the lord). Her Muslim father forbade her to dance as a shepherdess with the other schoolgirls. In that case, said the drama's director, we will cast you as Krishna. All you have to do is stand there in the usual Krishna pose, a flute at your mouth. Her father consented; and so the Muslim girl played Krishna.

This is India's "secularism." Indeed, Hindus pride themselves on belonging to a religion of astonishing breadth and range of belief; a religion that acknowledges all ways of worshipping God as equally valid—indeed, the only major religion in the world that does not claim to be the only true religion. This eclectic and nondoctrinaire Hinduism—a faith without apostasy, where there are no heretics to cast out because there has never been any such thing as a Hindu heresy—is not the Hinduism professed by those who destroyed a mosque, nor the Hindutva spewed in hate-filled speeches by communal politicians. How can such a religion lend itself to "fundamentalism"? Hindu fundamentalism is a contradiction in terms, since Hinduism is a religion without fundamentals. India has survived the Aryans, the Mughals, the British; it has taken from each—language, art, food, learning—and grown with all of them. To be an Indian is to be part of an elusive dream all Indians share, a dream that fills our minds with sounds, words, flavors from many sources that we cannot easily identify.

This is why the development of what has been called "Hindu fundamentalism" and the resultant change in the public discourse about Indianness is so dangerous. The suggestion that only a Hindu, and only a certain kind of Hindu, can be an authentic Indian is an affront to the very premise of Indian nationalism. The reduction of non-Hindus to second-class status in their homeland is unthinkable. It would be a second partition: and a partition in the Indian soul would be as bad as a partition in the Indian soil. The only possible idea of India is that of a nation greater than the sum of its parts.

Of course it is true that, while Hinduism as a faith might privilege tolerance, this does not necessarily mean that all Hindus behave tolerantly. Ironically, Hindu chauvinism has emerged from the competition for resources in a contentious democracy. Politicians of all faiths across India seek to mobilize voters by appealing to narrow identities; by seeking votes in the name of religion, caste, and region, they have urged voters to define themselves on these lines. As religion, caste, and region have come to dominate public discourse, to some it has become more important to be a Muslim, a Bodo, or a Yadav than to be an Indian. But this is not merely dangerous; it is an assault on the essential underpinnings of Indianness.

Yet India's democracy helps to acknowledge and accommodate the various identities of its multifaceted population. No one identity can ever triumph in India: both the country's chronic pluralism and the logic of the electoral marketplace make this impossible. In leading a coalition government, the Hindu-inclined Bharatiya Janata Party has learned that any party ruling India has to reach out to other groups, other interests, other minorities. After all, there are too many diversities in our land for any one version of reality to be imposed on all of us.

So the Indian identity celebrates diversity: if America is a melting pot, then to me India is a *thali,* a selection of sumptuous dishes in different bowls. Each tastes different, and does not necessarily mix with the next, but they belong together on the same plate, and they complement each other in making the meal a satisfying repast. Indians are used to multiple identities and multiple loyalties, all coming together in allegiance to a larger idea of India, an India that safeguards the common space available to each identity. That is the tradition to which Rushdie's "overartist" belonged.

At a time when the Huntington thesis of a "clash of civilizations" has gained currency, it is intriguing to contemplate a civilization predicated upon such diversity, one that provides the framework to absorb these clashes within itself. For Indians across the world, wary of the endless multiplication of sovereignties, hesitant before the clamor for division and self-assertion echoing in a hundred NRI (nonresident Indian) forums, this may be something to think about. In today's globalized world, Indians in Michigan cannot escape identification with what is happening to Indians in Mumbai. So the idea of India is an idea familiar to Americans but few others—of a land where it doesn't matter what the color of your skin is, the kind of food you eat, the sounds you make when you speak, the God you choose to worship (or not), so long as you want to play by the same rules as everybody else, and dream the same dreams. If the overwhelming majority of a people share the political will for unity, if they wear the dust of a shared history on their foreheads and the mud of an uncertain future on their feet, and if they realize they are better off in Kozhikode or Kanpur dreaming the same dreams as those in Kohlapur or Kohima, a nation exists, celebrating diversity and freedom—and that is the India to which Rushdie's overartist would belong.

To return, then, to Sonia Gandhi. Throughout its history the Congress Party has articulated and defended the idea that Indian nationalism is inclusive, tolerant, and pluralist, and that there are no acid tests of birth, religion, ethnicity, or even territory that disqualify one who wants to claim Indianness. As Ashutosh Varshney has pointed out, Sonia Gandhi "is an Indian—by her citizenship, by her act of living in India, and by the way she has adopted a new home. [A]n Indian is one who accepts the ethos of India." Some, like the Samata Party spokeswoman, have claimed that Sonia "will never be able to fully understand the intricacies of our culture" because "cultural impulses are gained in the early stages of life." This argument is preposterous, since some of the greatest experts on Indian culture, who have forgotten more than most Indians will ever know about *Bharatiya sanskriti*—from A. L. Basham to Richard Lannoy to R. C. Zaehner—are foreigners. Mani Shankar Aiyar turns the absurd "cultural" argument on its head by pointing out that "it is a disrespect to the millennial traditions of India to question the credentials of a daughter-in-law."

Sonia Gandhi herself has made her own case: "Though born in a foreign land, I chose India as my country," she points out. "I am Indian and shall remain so till my last breath. India is my motherland, dearer to me than my own life." But Sonia Gandhi is not the issue. Her personal fate is for her party, herself and above all the electorate to decide. The real issue is whether we should let politicians decide who is qualified to be an authentic Indian. India has always proclaimed "unity in diversity," the idea of one land embracing many. You can be fair-skinned, sari-wearing, and Italian-speaking, and you are not more foreign to my *ammamma* in Kerala than someone who is "wheatish-complexioned," wears a *salwar-kameez* and speaks Punjabi. Our nation absorbs both these types of people; both are equally "foreign" to some of us, equally Indian to us all. To start disqualifying Indian citizens from the privileges of Indianness is not just pernicious: it is an insult to the basic assumptions of Indian nationalism. An India that denies itself to some of us could end up being denied to all of us.

So who is an Indian? Anyone who wants to be, and is qualified by residence, allegiance, or citizenship. My India, like Salman Rushdie's, has room enough for everyone. In *The Moor's Last Sigh,* Moor (Moraes Zogoiby, the novel's narrator), celebrating his Catholic mother and Jewish father (and so referring to himself as a "cathjew nut"), has a metaphorical role as a symbol of Rushdie's India, a "unifier of opposites, a standard-bearer of pluralism," who in his mother's last paintings descends into "a semi-allegorical figure of decay." India is, as ever, not just a nation but a literary device, the intersection of the many strands of Rushdie's intellectual heritage—an eclectic palimpsest repeatedly painted over by history and myth, by colonial traders and settlers, by the English language, and by the tragic majesty of Islam, symbolized by the placing of the Alhambra on Bombay's Malabar Hill, the author's childhood address. The novel is suffused with nostalgia for an India much loved and, like Boabdil's Granada, lost (at the time of its writing, it must have seemed irretrievably lost) to the exiled writer. The sultan in *The Moor's Last Sigh* weeps for the world he has given up, for the history he has betrayed, the tradition he has failed to defend; he sighs for a loss that is intensely personal and yet of far greater significance than his own person. In this novel Rushdie too, through his own Moor, sighs upon his loss of the India he had known and loved and believed he might never be able to visit in safety again; but also for the greater loss of the secular, multireligious, pluriethnic India of which he has written with such passion and pride.

That India, though, still exists; it has not yet fallen to the bombs and the bigotry of the chauvinists and corrupt opportunists this novel excoriates. We need not spend much time on them; as Rushdie wrote of a Bombay building populated by the nouveau riche: "Everest Villas is twenty-nine stories high, but mercifully these are stories I do not need to tell." The Indian idea—that people of every imaginable color, creed, caste, cuisine, consonant, and conviction can live and strive and triumph together in one gloriously mongrel nation—is more relevant than ever, and it has no abler advocate than Salman Rushdie. He has become, as much for his convictions as for his creativity, the finest English writer of India, and the most gifted reinventor of Indianness since Nehru. Perhaps, as Rushdie himself has written, "the only people who see the whole picture are the ones who step out of the frame."

The "permeation of the real world by the fictional is a symptom of the moral decay of our postmillennial culture," declaims the anonymous narrator of one of the stories in Rushdie's collection *East West*. "There can be little doubt that a large majority of us opposes the free, unrestricted migration of imaginary beings into an already damaged reality, whose resources diminish by the day." Rushdie's tongue is of course firmly in his cheek here, but it is the free, unrestricted migration of his imagination that can help heal the tragic damage done to the reality of Indianness—an Indianness that his writing so remarkably celebrates.

A Response by Salman Rushdie

We live in the age of explanation and yet we understand each other less well every day. Open a newspaper, turn on the broadcast news, and an avalanche of explainers buries you under verbiage, telling you how to think about what you think you know. Science explains seven things a minute while religion claims to have explained everything already, anyway. The day passes to the sound of the powerful explaining away their mistakes, distortions, and lies. "Reality instructors," to use Bellow's term, are all around; reality instruction may be the biggest growth industry of our time. The bookstores are filled with nonfiction because we are losing faith in our dreams and believe that only the facts can tell the truth, but the most popular books of all are still fictions filled with the purest drivel. In our private lives we pay fortunes to sit in rooms with wiser men and women, seeking explanations for our weaknesses, our inner turbulence, our grief. We pay nobody, however, to help us understand our joys. These we can readily explain; or, rather, happiness needs no explanation. It is misery that demands a confessor.

In the midst of this dull riot of answers, is there still room for the bright questions of scholarly inquiry? And if we speak specifically about the arts, should we—or should we not—follow the advice of V. S. Naipaul, who once told an audience at the Hay-on-Wye literary festival that literature was not for the young, and recommended that all English departments in all universities should therefore be shut down immediately?

The relationship between the arts and their explainers has always been edgily ambiguous. It has been said that great writers need great critics, and there are instances—William Faulkner and Malcolm Cowley come to mind—when a critic's contribution to the understanding of a body of work has been essential. And where would surrealism be without André Breton. At the opposite end of this argument is Tom Wolfe, satirizing an art-culture in which theory precedes practice, and the *New York Times*'s chief art critic can write "to lack a persuasive theory is to lack something crucial"; so that, as Wolfe says, *"the paintings . . . exist only to illustrate the text."* Several years ago, I was at a British

Council literary seminar in Walberberg, Germany, where a group of well-known British authors (Ian McEwan, James Fenton, Caryl Phillips among them) shocked an audience of eminent European scholars and critics by claiming that all the work done studying and explicating their books was not of much interest to them, and could not be described as useful or helpful.

I wondered, at the time, if we writers were telling the truth, or simply taking up an essentially defensive (though apparently aggressive) position. In the aftermath of the Death of the Author, after all, it is the Critic who is king, and yet there we were, obstinately alive, and determined to retain sovereignty over our own texts. As time passes, however, I admit to having more and more difficulty with this whole business of being Explained, rather than merely—happily—read.

The trouble begins with having to explain oneself. When I publish a book my strong instinct is to absent myself completely, because at the moment of publication the writer's time with the book is at an end, and the reader's time begins. You offer up your tale and then you want to hear from other people; the least interesting voice, at that moment, is your own. However—for such is the nature of the publishing industry—at the very moment when the author wishes to be invisible, he is required to be most visible. Every writer comes to dread the sound of his own voice repeating answers over and over again. The effect, if the process goes on long enough (and it does, it does) is to alienate one from one's own work. Publication comes to seem like the process by which the author is persuaded to detest his book, so that he has to begin writing another story to obliterate the one he can no longer bear to discuss.

In my own case, these antiexplanatory feelings were intensified by the strange hubbub that followed the publication of *The Satanic Verses*. Rarely, if ever, can any author have been called upon to explicate his own book so frequently, in such detail, and often in the face of entrenched, often hostile attitudes toward the text that were based upon not reading it, or reading a few bits of it (sentences carefully selected and decontextualized to create a "meaning" that bore no relationship to the "meaning" of the book as a whole), or vindictively misreading it, or reading it through the transforming lenses of assumptions about religion and its privileges, about "culture" (that much-abused word) and its "sensitivities," and, of course about me—assumptions and prejudices that, for many readers, turned the book, and its author, into entities unworthy of serious consideration. You didn't need to read *The Satanic Verses* to hold an opinion about it, because the clamor of angry explanations told you it wasn't worth the trouble. "I don't need to walk in the gutter," said one such nonreader critic, "to know that it contains filth." You didn't need to concern yourself about the book's author, either, because the same clamor told you how unpleasant a person he was.

To fight back against this assault it was necessary to say, over and over again, what I thought my book was about, and to explain why I had written it in the way I had written it and not in some other, less problematic way; to explain, indeed, why I had written it at all, when not writing it would plainly have been so much less troublesome to everyone. It often felt that I was also required to offer up a similar exegesis of "Salman Rushdie." Instead of discussing themes, ideas, characters, feelings, language, form, tone, I had to justify my right to write at all. "He knew what he was doing," people said, but nobody actually cared what that was. So I had to spell it out, again and again. None of this was pleasant. All of it felt necessary.

I have been obliged by extraordinary circumstances to do what I believe that a writer should never do: to try and impose my own reading of my work upon the world, to prescribe its meanings, to say clearly what was intended by each contested paragraph, to try and establish the work as proper, justifiable, moral, perhaps even good, in the face of an onslaught that insisted it was improper, unjustifiable, immoral, and bad. In general it is my view that the reader completes the book; that one of the joys of literature is that each reading will be different, because of what each reader brings to the experience. It is my view that it is not for the author to tell the reader how to read his work. And yet there I have been, in interview after interview, and in many written pieces, trying to rescue my work from its detractors, and saying, in effect, "This is what this passage means," or, "Read this part like this."

Even today, twenty-two years after I began to write *The Satanic Verses,* I am still asked for detailed accounts of the day-to-day motivations of writing its many sentences. The truthful answer ("I don't remember") is, of course, unsatisfactory. So I have come up with my little bunch of answers, answers that satisfy some questioners—not, evidently, the ones who will never be satisfied—but which increasingly trouble me. I, too, am a reality instructor now. You only have to read the interviews with me that appear in this volume to appreciate that. How readily I fall into the trap of explaining my motives, my characters, my sentences; how willingly I talk about ideas and controversies, attacks and defenses! What book, what body of work could retain the slightest aura of mystery when the author himself shines such a bright light on its origins amd meanings? Why won't that garrulous author be quiet and let his books speak for themselves?

I once saw Joseph Heller being interviewed about, if memory serves, his novel *Good as Gold*, and refusing, in spite of much coaxing by the interviewer, to talk about his book in any terms except those of his characters: what they felt, what they wanted, what they were like, why they acted as they did. He simply refused to step back from his art and pontificate about it "from the outside." How wise he was! *Why can't I do that?*

None of the above observations should be understood to mean that I am anything but deeply grateful for the intensive, close, spirited readings offered in this collection. Ashutosh Varshney and Husain Haqqani, dealing with Pakistani aspects of my work, offer much historical insight and, in both cases, some perhaps surprising contemporary optimism about the future of Indo-Pak relations, the Kashmir issue, and Pakistan itself. (However, now that we have heard President Musharraf and his Indian counterparts begin to speak of the possibility of abolishing the Line of Control and jointly guaranteeing the integrity of a semiautonomous and reunified Kashmir, it may be that they will be proved right.) Haqqani very usefully offers an account of the nature of the attack on *The Satanic Verses* in Pakistan, and begins, too, that process of "reimagining Pakistan" without which no good future for that country can be proposed. Shashi Tharoor's insights, not only into my work but more generally into the nature and value of Indian secularism, are, I think, extremely important; Sara Suleri Goodyear's analysis of veil images in my books has acquired a new relevance because of the recent igniting of a debate over the wearing of the veil by Muslim women in Western countries. I am also delighted to see "my" Bombay, both the childhood Bombay that gave birth to *Midnight's Children* and the adult Mumbai out of which *The Moor's Last Sigh* was created, so thoroughly understood, opened up, and explored as they are in Thomas Blom Hansen's "Reflections." And Akeel Bilgrami's insistence on defending *The Satanic Verses* with an "internalist" argument chimes profoundly with my own, obstinate feeling—that I never set out to insult anybody, that the novel contains an extremely sympathetic portrait of a Muslim (and non-Muslim, South Asian) community wrestling with the consequences of transcultural migration; and that to engage with the core stories and ideas of a religion and wrestle with them, even from a modern, nonreligious viewpoint, is a serious act, the opposite of "offensive." At the height of the controversy I longed for someone to offer this kind of "quality defense," not just a defense based on free-speech principles but one that took on board the intention, argument, and yes, the achievement of the book. I'm glad to have such an argument offered at last.

It would be churlish, after so many kinds of intellectual generosity by these writers, to linger overmuch on the inevitable "buts" of criticism. Akeel Bilgrami distances himself from what he thinks my opinions on U.S. foreign policy to be, and Sara Suleri worries about what she calles a "self-parodic mode" in my more recent novels. In point of fact I suspect my views about Afghanistan and Iraq are not so very far from Bilgrami's, and as for *The Ground beneath Her Feet,* I shall just have to take Suleri's opinion on the chin and allow others, elsewhere, to stand up for the book.

There is perhaps just one proposition with which I must briefly engage. Bilgrami, resisting a "universal conclusion about the rationality of free speech," appears to be sliding away from the First Amendment position. To my mind, however, the best argument in favor of the principle of the universality of free speech is not an appeal to its rationality, but to its place at the heart of human nature. We are, as I've often said, *storytelling animals,* the only creatures on our planet, as far as we know, that use story—narrative, history, gossip, philosophy—as a way of understanding ourselves. Any external limitations on our ability to speak, or on the content of our speech, therefore interferes with something essential to us all, whether we are writers or not. When people are told that they cannot freely reexamine the stories of themselves, and the stories within which they live, then tyranny is not very far away.

Contributors

Akeel Bilgrami is the Johnsonian Professor of Philosophy and the Director of the Heyman Center for the Humanities at Columbia University. He is also a member of Columbia's Committee on Global Thought. He got a first degree in English literature from Bombay University; studied philosophy, politics, and economics at Oxford as a Rhodes Scholar; and earned a Ph.D. from the University of Chicago. He joined Columbia University in 1985 after spending two years as an assistant professor at the University of Michigan, Ann Arbor. His publications include the following books: *Belief and Meaning* (1992); *Self-Knowledge and Resentment* (2006); and *What Is a Muslim?* and *Politics and the Moral Psychology of Identity*, both due in 2008. He has published over sixty articles in *Philosophy of Mind* as well as in *Political and Moral Psychology*. Some of his articles in these latter publications speak to issues of current politics in their relation to broader social and cultural issues.

Sara Suleri Goodyear is the author of the memoir *Meatless Days* (1989) and *The Rhetoric of English India* (1992), a scholarly book. Her interests include postcolonial literatures and theory, contemporary cultural criticism, literature and law, Romantic and Victorian poetry, and Edmund Burke. She was a founding editor of the *Yale Journal of Criticism* (*YJC*) and serves on the editorial boards of *YJC*, the *Yale Review,* and *Transition.*

Thomas Blom Hansen is Professor of Anthropology and the Director of the Graduate School of Social Sciences at the University of Amsterdam. His recent books include *The Saffron Wave: Democracy and Hindu Nationalism in Modern India* (1999) and *Wages of Violence: Naming and Identity in Postcolonial Bombay* (2001). He has more recently coedited (with F. Stepputat) *Sovereign Bodies: Citizens, Migrants, and States in the Postcolonial World* (2005). At present he is completing a book on the experience of postapartheid freedom in South Africa through the eyes of residents of a formerly Indian township in Durban.

Husain Haqqani has served Pakistan as a journalist, professor, and diplomat. He has been a columnist for *Asian Wall Street Journal,* the *Indian Express,* and *Gulf News,* among other newspapers; a professor at Boston University; and is currently Pakistan's ambassador to the United States. In the 1990s, he served as Pakistan's High Commissioner to Sri Lanka.

Daniel Herwitz is the Director of the Institute for the Humanities and Mary Fair Croushore Professor of the Humanities at the University of Michigan, where he also holds professorships in comparative literature, philosophy, and history of art. Before coming to Michigan Herwitz lived and worked in South Africa, where he was Chair in Philosophy at the University of Natal (1996–2002) and Director of the Center for Knowledge and Innovation there. His book of essays, *Race and Reconciliation* (2003), is the result of that stay. Herwitz has published widely in aesthetics, most recently *The Star as Icon* (2008) and *Aesthetics: Key Concepts in Philosophy* (2008). His collaboration with the Indian painter M. F. Husain led to the book *Husain* (Tata Press, 1988), which won a National Book Award in India.

Salman Rushdie is the author of ten novels, one collection of short stories, and four works of nonfiction and the coeditor of *The Vintage Book of Indian Writing*. In 1993 *Midnight's Children* was judged to be the Booker of Bookers, the best novel to have won the Booker Prize in its first twenty-five years. *The Moor's Last Sigh* won the Whitbread Prize in 1995 and the European Union's Aristeion Prize for Literature in 1996. He is a Fellow of the Royal Society of Literature and a Commandeur des Arts et des Lettres. He was knighted in June 2007.

Dr. Shashi Tharoor is Chairman of Dubai-based Afras Ventures; a prizewinning author of ten books, both fiction and nonfiction; and a widely published critic, commentator, and columnist (including for the *Hindu*, the *Times of India*, and *Newsweek*). In 2007 he concluded a nearly twenty-nine-year career with the United Nations, including working for refugees in South-East Asia at the peak of the "boat people" crisis, handling peacekeeping operations in the former Yugoslavia, and culminating as the Under-Secretary-General for Communications and Public Information. In 2006, he was India's candidate to succeed Kofi Annan as UN Secretary-General and emerged a strong second out of seven contenders. His books include the classic *The Great Indian Novel* (1989); *India: From Midnight to the Millennium* (1997); *Nehru: The Invention of India* (2003); and most recently, *The Elephant, the Tiger, and the Cell Phone: Reflections on India, the Emerging 21st-Century Power* (2007). Dr. Tharoor earned his Ph.D. at the Fletcher School of Law and Diplomacy at the age of twenty-two and was named by the World Economic Forum in Davos in 1998 as a "Global Leader of Tomorrow." He was awarded the Pravasi Bharatiya Samman, India's highest honor for overseas Indians. [For more on Shashi Tharoor, please see www.shashitharoor.com.] He is married to Christa, a Canadian who is Deputy Secretary of the United Nations Disarmament Commission, and is the father of twin sons, Ishaan and Kanishk.

Ashutosh Varshney is Professor of Political Science, University of Michigan, Ann Arbor. Previously, he was on the faculty of Harvard University for nine years. Born in India and trained at Allahabad and Jawaharlal Nehru Universities in India before coming to the United States, he earned his Ph.D. from MIT. His research and teaching cover three areas: ethnicity and nationalism, political economy of development, and South Asian politics and political economy. His books include *Ethnic Conflict and Civic Life: Hindus and Muslims in India* (2002), which won the Gregory Luebbert Prize of the American Political Science Association and was a Kiriyama Prize "notable" in 2003; *Democracy, Development, and the Countryside: Urban-Rural Struggles in India* (1995), which won the Daniel Lerner prize at MIT in 1990; and *India's Democracy and Its Unfinished Quests* (forthcoming). In addition, he has published over thirty academic papers in various professional journals. He has also contributed occasionally to the *Financial Times, Newsweek, Indian Express*, the *Times of India, India Today, Outlook,* and *Far Eastern Economic Review*. He is a 2008 winner of the Guggenheim Fellowship and the Carnegie Scholar awards and has in the past received fellowships from the Ford and MacArthur Foundations, Open Society Institute, Social Science Research Council, and Woodrow Wilson Center for International Scholars. He served on UN Secretary-General Kofi Annan's Task Force on Millennium Development Goals (2002–5).

Gauri Viswanathan is Class of 1933 Professor of English and Comparative Literature at Columbia University. She is the author of *Masks of Conquest: Literary Study and British Rule in India* (1989; 2nd ed., 1998) and *Outside the Fold: Conversion, Modernity, and Belief* (1998), which won, among other prizes, the James Russell Lowell Prize awarded by the Modern Language Association of America. She is also the editor of *Power, Politics, and Culture: Interviews with Edward W. Said* (2001). She has published widely in education, religion, and culture; nineteenth-century British and colonial cultural studies; and the history of modern disciplines. Her current book in progress, *In Search of Blavatsky,* is on modern occultism and the writing of alternative religious histories.

Index